100 ANCIENT CHINESE CUSTOMS

中國古代風俗一百則

一百叢書㉒

漢英對照 Chinese-English

厲振儀 編著　姚紅 英譯

100
ANCIENT
CHINESE CUSTOMS
中國古代風俗
一百則

臺 灣 商 務 印 書 館 發 行

《一百叢書》總序

　　本館出版英漢（或漢英）對照《一百叢書》的目的，是希望憑藉着英、漢兩種語言的對譯，把中國和世界各類著名作品的精華部分介紹給中外讀者。

　　本叢書的涉及面很廣。題材包括了寓言、詩歌、散文、短篇小說、書信、演說、語錄、神話故事、聖經故事、成語故事、名著選段等等。

　　顧名思義，《一百叢書》中的每一種都由一百個單元組成。以一百為單位，主要是讓編譯者在浩瀚的名著的海洋中作挑選時有一個取捨的最低和最高限額。至於取捨的標準，則是見仁見智，各有心得。

　　由於各種書中被選用的篇章節段，都是以原文或已被認定的範本作藍本，而譯文又經專家學者們精雕細琢，千錘百煉，故本叢書除可作為各種題材的精選讀本外，也是研習英漢兩種語言對譯的理想參考書，部分更可用作朗誦教材。外國學者如要研習漢語，本書亦不失為理想工具。

商務印書館 (香港) 有限公司

編輯部

前　言

　　這本《中國古代風俗一百則》實際是我從事中國民俗課教學的一點心得。這些年，我在上海外國語大學一邊教對外漢語專業的中國民俗學課，一邊給外國留學生上民俗（事象）課。我覺得由於民俗真切而具體地表現了一個民族的倫理觀念、道德標準、價值取向和審美情趣，中國學生可從中增加對自己民族文化的理解，更加關注和熱愛身邊的一切；外國留學生則通過了解民間風俗，擴大對中華民族的感性知識。而民俗課亦提高了留學生的跨文化交際技能。多年來，我因教學需要涉獵了大量古代參考書籍，每當我興趣盎然地閱讀這些資料時，將它們介紹給讀者的念頭便油然而生。不謀而合，香港商務印書館《一百叢書》的編者邀我編寫這本書，這使我特別高興。企盼讀者能通過本書也對中國的民間風俗產生濃厚的興趣，並有所得益。

　　作為代代相傳的一種文化現象，民間風俗的傳承性特徵是顯而易見的。我們可以發現，本書中所介紹的大多數風俗習慣，有的傳承於千年以前，有的沿襲了幾百年，在現實生活中仍鮮活地存在着。儘管歷史變遷，儘管南北東西有地域差異，我們今天的很多風俗在主要內容和形式上與古代相差無幾。

　　中國民間風俗是由中國獨特的地理環境、社會歷史環境、文化傳統造就的，因而它呈現出鮮明的民族特點。居住、服飾、飲食等物質方面的習俗固然最能體現中國風俗的民族特徵，然而民族的心態，如對團圓美滿的注重和追求，不獨在除夕、元宵、中秋等這些強調家人團聚的歲時節日中反映出來，也能在企盼"花好月圓"的生活而產生的諸如傳袋求子、撒帳祝吉、合髻、合卺等婚俗中充分說明。此外，儘管中國民間迷信神佛的觀念十分牢固，但人們卻不篤信某一神靈，而往往從功利實用的目的出發崇拜多神，因而關公誕盛況空前，西湖香市也熱鬧非凡；商店民居中將不屬同一神系的彌勒、財神、壽星、關公等的神象供於一案進香膜拜的景象至今仍隨處可見。廣泛的實用性是中國風俗的另一個特點：夏初端午節懸艾和菖蒲驅五毒的習俗、近歲末冬至撣塵的節令衛生習俗，都蘊含着一定的科學道理；元宵觀燈、端午龍舟競渡、重陽登高具有娛樂健身的作用；而一些古老的懷孕生產育兒的習俗則包含了對婦女和兒童的保護作用。實用性也是一些良俗得以代代相傳的重要原因。原始的神秘性又是中國民間風俗的一個特點：帶着猙獰面具的儺舞儺戲起源古老；為死者超度亡靈的"做七"、"做陰壽"等習俗勾勒出人鬼交流的渠道；信仰、祭祀、占卜、禁忌等習俗中，更充分顯示這神秘原始的特色。此外，由於幾千年封建思想的統治，中國的民間風俗如封建禮法、男尊女卑等封建觀念都在婚姻喪葬、人生儀禮習俗方面較集中地顯露出來。

本書從幾十種古籍中選取了一百則有關古代風俗的內容，將它們譯成白話，並配以英譯，故亦是一本文言白話對照，漢英對照的語言學習讀物。一百則由六大方面的內容組成：歲時節日習俗 (1-23)、婚喪孕產育兒習俗 (24-43)、信仰崇拜禁忌習俗 (44-62)、交際娛樂習俗與社會風情 (63-88)、服飾飲食建築習俗 (89-96)、商貿習俗 (97-100)。雖限於篇幅，還有許多資料未能使用，然一斑可窺全豹，中國古代人們的物質及精神生活在這一百則中仍可給我們許多啟迪。

　　本書的英譯文是由我的同事姚紅女士承擔的。這一期間她正遠在美國執教，相隔萬里，我倆雖是第一次合作，但相當愉快。美國 City Grove 大學的 William Donnelly 教授給了本書英譯文許多指正，在此我們表示深深的感謝。

厲振儀
1996年7月於上海

Preface

One Hundred Ancient Chinese Customs is the fruit of the many years of my teaching Chinese Folklore to students majoring in Teaching Chinese as a Foreign Language and to classes in Chinese Folklore for International Students. Folk customs manifest many aspects of a people: its culture, ethical concepts, moral standards, values and aesthetic principles. Chinese students studying their own traditions and customs can acquire a deeper understanding of their nation's culture and as a result develop an appreciation and care for what is happening around them. International students taking a course in Chinese customs can deepen their insights into Chinese life and enhance their ability to communicate interculturally. As a teacher, I have over the years surveyed many classic folklore compilations. As I have become more engrossed in the study of these ancient writings, my natural response has been a strong wish to share them with other readers. When The Commercial Press editors invited me to compile this book for their *One Hundred Series*, I was delighted as I could fulfil my long-term desire to promote an interest in and an appreciation of folk customs among the readers.

Folk customs, practices that have been passed down from generation to generation, constitute a valuable set of cultural heirlooms. In this book, the reader will find that many folkways and mores, still observed in our daily life, can be traced back hundreds, or even thousands, of years. Despite the vicissitudes in history and despite regional variations, many of the customs we observe today do not differ materially from those of ancient times.

Chinese folk customs are formed under unique Chinese geographical, social and historical environments and cultural traditions. They therefore exhibit distinctive national characteristics. While customs involving accommodation, clothing and feeding can best illustrate the uniqueness of the material culture of the Chinese nation, the importance attached to and the pursuit of reunion and happiness in seasonal festivals emphasizing family reunion, such as the New Year's Eve Vigil, the Lantern Festival and the Mid-Autumn Festival, can well reflect the mentality and spirit of the Chinese people. We can also feel this distinctive spirit in matrimonial customs inspired by the desire for a life of "blooming flowers and full moons (perfect conjugal bliss)", customs such as passing over bags as a quest for an offspring, showering coins and dried fruit on newlyweds as a blessing, knotting the bride's with the bridegroom's hair and drinking the wedding cup.

On the other hand, despite a penchant for blind faith in deities and devotion to Buddhas, the Chinese people do not limit their devotion to just one deity or spirit. Instead, they are practical enough to worship a variety of deities.

Consequently, whereas the birthday of Master Guan is a grand occasion, the incense-stick market in the West Lake for the worship of other gods also becomes a scene of bustle and excitement. In stores and ordinary households, one can easily find people offering sacrifices to different types of deities all at the same shrine, for example, Maitreya, the God of Wealth, the Longevity Star and Master Guan. Basic practicality is another characteristic of Chinese folk customs. Hanging Chinese mugwort and calamus by the door in the Dragon Boat Festival to dispel the "five pests", or the seasonal hygienic habit of dusting at the Winter Soltice, customs involving sanitation, are scientifically grounded. Displaying lanterns during the Lantern Festival, racing boats in the Dragon Boat Festival, climbing mountains on the Double Ninth — these practices have functions of entertainment and physical exercise. Some ancient pregnancy, delivery and child-rearing customs function to protect women and children. In fact, practicality is an important factor in the survival of many beneficial customs passed on from generation to generation.

Yet another characteristic of Chinese folk customs is their primeval mysticism. *Nuo* dancing with hideous masks originated in very ancient times. Liberating souls from purgatory involves such practices of observing the "sevenths" and celebrating "nether birthdays". These practices provide channels for the living to communicate with the dead.

Mysticism manifests itself most distinctively in superstitions, sacrificial ceremonies, divinations and taboos. Moreover, because of thousands of years of domination by feudalistic ideology, Chinese folk customs often assume feudal characteristics. Feudal protocol and ideas, such as male superiorty, find expression in marriage and funeral ceremonies and other social rites.

This book is a selection of a hundred examples of ancient Chinese customs from dozens of classical works. They are rewritten in modern Chinese and in English. Therefore this book is also a practical reader presenting texts in ancient Chinese, modern Chinese and English. The hundred pieces are classified in six categories:

— customs of seasonal festivals (Passages 1-23);

— customs of marriage, funeral, pregnancy, delivery and child-rearing (Passages 24-43);

— customs concerning beliefs, worship and taboo (Passages 44-62);

— customs of socialization (Passages 63-88);

— customs involving clothing, food and architecture (Passages 89-96), and

— customs of commerce and trade (Passages 97-100).

Owing to limited space, this selection is only a fraction of the abundance of material. However, as the Chinese saying goes, "one can visualize a leopard from its spots", these hundred passages provide a glimpse of the material and spiritual life of the ancient Chinese people, which is inspiring.

The translation of this book was undertaken by my colleague Ms.Yao Hong, who during this period is teaching in the United States. Though separated by thousands of miles, we found this first cooperation of ours very pleasant. Here, we would like to express our heartfelt gratitude to Dr. William Donnelly of Grove City College who offered much valuable advice on the translation.

Li Zhenyi
Shanghai, May 1996.

目　錄

CONTENTS

一 貼春聯 [1]

春聯者,即桃符 [2] 也。自入臘以後,即有文人墨客 [3],在市肆檐下,書寫春聯,以圖潤筆 [4]。祭竈 [5] 之後,漸次黏掛,千門萬戶,煥然一新。

清 富察敦崇《燕京歲時記》

【語譯】

春聯,就是桃符。進入夏曆十二月,就有一些讀書人在市場店舖的屋檐下書寫對聯,以此獲得報酬。祭竈神 [十二月廿三或廿四日] 以後,人們陸陸續續地把春聯張貼起來。眾多人家 [的大門上],[頓時] 煥然一新。

【註釋】

1. 貼春聯:春節時把寫在紅紙上的聯語貼在門上。此風俗流行於中國各地。源於在桃木板上題寫聯語的風俗。參見第五十三篇"桃木驅邪"。
2. 桃符:古代春節民間用兩塊桃木板懸掛在門上,上畫兩門神像或書寫聯語,藉以驅鬼壓邪。明代以後改寫在紙上。
3. 文人墨客:指讀書人。
4. 潤筆:付給作詩、畫書畫之人的報酬。
5. 祭竈:參見第二十三篇"送竈神"。

2

1 Putting up the Spring Scrolls[1]

Spring scrolls were originally called *tao fu*[2]. Commencing with lunar December some scholars began to write these scrolls under the eaves of the market stalls to earn some extra money. New scrolls were gradually posted, after the ceremonial sacrifices to the Kitchen God[3], on doors, house after house, giving the neighbourhood a fresh look.

Fucha Duncong (Qing Dynasty):
<u>Annual Records of the Capital</u>

Notes:

1. Putting up the spring scrolls: In the lunar new year, it is a custom to post couplets written on red paper on doors. This is practised in all parts of China. It originated from the custom of writing charms on peach wood. (See Passage 53)

2. *tao fu*: In ancient times, during the Spring Festival, people hung up two peachwood plaques on their doors. On the peach wood were either a pair of portraits of the Door God or a couplet. Both were intended to drive away evil spirits. After the Ming Dynasty the spells were written on sheets of paper which were called spring scrolls.

3. Kitchen God: See Passage 23.

二　除夕[1]

　　士庶家不論大小，俱打掃門閭，去塵穢，淨庭戶，換門神[2]，掛鍾馗[3]，釘桃符，貼春牌[4]；祭祀祖宗。遇夜則備迎神香花[5]供物，以祈新歲之安。

　　　　　　　　　　　宋　吳自牧《夢粱錄》

【語譯】

　　士大夫家和普通老百姓家，不論社會地位高低，[在除夕這一天]都要打掃大門，除去塵埃，把庭院門窗洗滌得乾乾淨淨，換上新的門神，掛上鍾馗的像，釘上桃符，貼上春聯，以及祭祀祖宗。到晚上就要準備香、花和供物迎神，以祈求新年平安。

【註釋】

1. 除夕：夏曆十二月最後一天，也稱“大年夜”、“年三十”。中國人一年中的盛大節日。
2. 門神：流行於全中國廣大地區的新年習俗。人們把兩位門神的像貼在大門口的兩扇門上，以為可以把守門庭，不讓惡鬼進門，保護家中人畜平安。
3. 鍾馗：傳說中專門捉鬼的神靈。
4. 春牌：指春聯。
5. 香花：香和花是佛教禮敬儀式上必需用的東西。

2 Chinese New Year's Eve

All the folk, nobles and commoners alike, clean up their houses and their yards on Chinese New Year's Eve. They also put up a new portrait of the Door God[1] and a portrait of Zhong Kui[2], and glue on spring scrolls or nail up an inscribed peachwood plaque. They offer sacrifices to their ancestors, too. When evening comes, they prepare joss sticks, fresh flowers and offerings to welcome divinities and pray for a peaceful new year.

Wu Zimu (Song Dynasty):
Records of a Pipe Dream

Notes:

1. Door God: The custom of putting up a portrait of the Door God is practised in all parts of China during the New Year celebrations. The portrait is posted on the door of the main entrance to guard the house against evil spirits and protect all living beings in the house.

2. Zhong Kui: a legendary spirit which specializes in catching and consuming ghosts.

三　合家歡、守歲[1]

除夜，家庭舉宴，長幼咸集，多作吉利語。名曰“年夜飯[2]”，俗呼“合家歡”。……

家人圍爐團坐，小兒嬉戲，通宵不眠，謂之守歲。……燃雙椽燭于寢室中，宵永燭長，生花報喜，紅榮四照，直接晨光，謂之“守歲燭”。

清　顧祿《清嘉錄》

【語譯】

夏曆十二月三十日晚上，家家準備了豐盛的晚飯，[全家]大小、長輩、小輩聚集在一起[吃晚飯]，[席間]大家不時地說[一些祝福新年的]吉利話，這叫“年夜飯”，俗稱“合家歡”。

全家人圍着火爐坐，孩子們遊戲玩耍，[除夕夜]通宵不睡，這被稱之“守歲”。……在臥室中點一對[大]蠟燭，夜漫漫，燭焰修長，燭芯中結成的花狀物是報喜[的象徵]，紅光照亮了四方，直到晨曦[微露]。這就是[除夕夜的]“守歲燭”。

3 Happy Family Reunion Dinner[1] and New Year's Eve Vigil[2]

On the Chinese New Year's Eve, sumptuous banquets are prepared in each household. All the family members, young and old, sit around the table. While at dinner, they repeatedly express good wishes for the new year. This feast is called the New Year's Eve Dinner, commonly known as the Happy Family Reunion Dinner.

People stay awake throughout the Chinese New Year's Eve. All the older family members sit around the fireplace as the children play games. This is the New Year's Eve Vigil. A pair of big candles are lit in the bedroom, their slender flames lighting up the long night. A flower-like ash formed by the candlewick presages good luck. The auspicious red candlelight illuminates the surroundings until the first rays of the morning sun appear.

Gu Lu (Qing Dynasty):
Worthy Records of the Qing Dynasty

【註釋】

1. 守歲：流行於中國各地的歲末習俗。除夕夜吃罷年夜飯，點燃香燭，全家人團坐在一起，邊聊天邊吃瓜果點心，或做遊戲，直至深夜或黎明。含有送舊迎新，祝父母長壽之意。

2. 年夜飯：也稱“團圓飯”。不僅菜肴豐富，而且都具祈求吉利的含義。通常要家庭成員到齊了才開始吃。

Notes:

1. The Happy Family Reunion Dinner: or the New Year's Eve Dinner. The sumptuous dishes at this dinner all have auspicious meanings. Dinner starts only when all the family members have arrived.

2. The New Year's Eve Vigil: called *shou sui*, is a custom popularly practised in all parts of China. After the New Year's Eve dinner, all the family members sit around with the candles lit, eating fruit and snacks and playing games until late at night or early in the morning. This custom signifies ringing out the old year and ringing in the new. It also expresses wishes for the longevity of parents in the family.

四　辭歲[1]

　　凡除夕，蟒袍補褂[2]走親友者，謂之辭歲。家長叩見尊長，也曰辭歲。新婚者必至岳家辭歲，否則為不恭。

清　富察敦崇《燕京歲時記》

【語譯】

　　通常，除夕那天穿着盛裝走訪親友，即稱為"辭歲"。一家之長去拜見[比自己]輩份高的人，也說是"辭歲"。新婚的男人一定要去岳父家辭歲，否則就是不禮貌的。

【註釋】

1. 辭歲：也稱辭年，舊時流行於中國多數地區的習俗。含有告別舊年，迎接新年之意。
2. 蟒袍補褂：明清時代官員的服裝。

4 Ringing out the Old Year[1]

Usually on the Chinese New Year's Eve, people dress up to visit relatives and friends. The eldest in the family pays a formal visit to his senior relatives. This practice is called "saying goodbye to the old year". New sons-in-law must also visit their fathers-in-law lest they be regarded as disrespectful.

Fucha Duncong (Qing Dynasty):
Annual Records of the Capital

Notes:

1. Ringing out the old year: A custom popularly practised in many parts of China in the old days. It signifies ringing out the old year and ringing in the new.

五　分壓歲錢[1]

長者殆小兒，以朱繩綴百錢，謂之壓歲錢。置桔荔[2]諸果于枕畔，謂之壓歲果子。元旦睡覺時食之，取讖[3]于吉利，為新年休徵。

清　顧祿《清嘉錄》

【語譯】

[除夕夜，] 長輩送給小孩用紅色繩子穿起的百個錢幣，稱為壓歲錢。把桔子、荔枝等各種果子放在 [孩子的] 枕邊，這稱為"壓歲果"。元旦那天睡覺的時候吃了，[人們] 把這作為吉利的標誌，是新年吉祥的徵兆。

【註釋】

1. 壓歲錢：除夕夜，吃年夜飯以後，長輩向晚輩分發壓歲錢，據説能壓邪驅鬼。舊時用紅繩穿編成串，現多用小紅紙袋封盛。漢語中"歲"與"祟"(祟：鬼怪)諧音，"壓歲"即是"壓祟"。

2. 桔、荔：與"吉利"諧音，所以把這兩種水果放在孩子的枕邊。

3. 讖：預兆。

5   Distributing *Ya Sui* Money[1]

On New Year's Eve, the elder members of a family would string together a hundred copper coins on red twine as a gift for the children. This gift is called "*ya sui* money". People also place fruits like tangerines and lychees[2] by the side of the children's pillows. These are called "*ya sui* fruits". Children eat them before going to bed on New Year's night. This is regarded as an auspicious practice which promises good luck in the new year.

Gu Lu (Qing Dynasty):
<u>*Worthy Records of the Qing Dynasty*</u>

Notes:

1. *Ya sui* money: In Chinese, the word "*sui*" (year) is homonymic with the word "*sui*" (demon). Thus, "*ya sui*" is interpreted as suppressing demons — "*ya*": suppressing, and "*sui*": evil.
    After the New Year's Eve dinner, the senior members of the family distribute *ya sui* money to the children. It is believed that this practice can help to suppress evil and drive away demons. The red string of copper coins is now replaced by money sealed in red envelopes.

2. tangerines and lychees: In Chinese, these two words put together are homonymic with the word "auspicious".

六　新年放爆竹[1]

　　正月一日是三元之日也。《春秋》謂之端月。雞鳴而起，先于庭前放爆竹，以辟山臊[2]惡鬼。

　　按：《神異經》云：西方山中有人焉，其長尺餘，一足，性不畏人，犯之則令人寒熱，名曰山臊；以竹著火中，熚爆有聲，而山臊驚憚。《元黃經》所謂山臊[3]鬼也。

　　俗人以為爆竹起于庭燎，家國[4]不應濫于王者。

南朝梁　宗懍《荊楚歲時記》

【語譯】

　　正月初一是一年、四季、十二月開始的第一天。《春秋傳》稱正月叫端月。[人們] 在雄雞叫的時候就起身，先在堂階前燒響竹筒，用來驅趕 [一種名叫] 山臊的惡鬼。

　　按語：《神異經》上說：西方山上有 [一種怪] 人，它高一尺多，一只腳，生性不怕人。如果觸犯它，它就讓人發冷發熱，[這種怪人] 名叫山臊。把竹子放到火中燒，發出嗶嗶剝剝的聲音，山臊就吃驚害怕了。這是《元黃經》上所說到的山臊鬼。

　　一般人認為，爆竹起源於 [帝王庭中用於照明的]火炬。諸侯和普通老百姓不該濫用君王 [這種儀式]。

6 Firecrackers[1] on New Year's Day

The first day of the first lunar month is the first day of the year, of the season and of the twelve months. In Stories of Spring and Autumn, it is called Duan Yue, the beginning of the month. On that day, people get up at cockcrow. They light firecrackers in the yard to drive away the *shan sao*, the legendary ghosts that haunt the mountains.

According to the Book of Fairies and Ghosts, a strange creature dwells in the western mountains. It is single-legged and a little over a foot tall. By nature, it is unafraid of human beings. If offended, it will afflict the offender with fever. It is called the *shan sao*. To scare it, people burn bamboo which bursts with a popping sound. In The Book of Yuan Huang, this creature is called "the *shan chao* ghost".

People believe that the practice of burning bamboo originated from the lighting of torches in the royal palace. So it is thought that mere nobles and ordinary people should not adopt this royal practice.

Zong Lin (Southern Dynasties, the State of Liang):
Stories of the Jing and Chu Times

【註釋】

1. 爆竹：古代燒竹筒子叫"爆竹"。宋代以後才有捲紙裹着炸藥的爆竹，這也稱為"爆仗"。在新年或喜慶日放爆竹，是流傳至今的習俗。

2. 山臊：傳說中住在山中的惡鬼。也寫作"山魈"。

3. 山魈：即山臊。

4. 家國：在這兒泛指諸侯與普通老百姓。

Notes:

1. firecrackers: In ancient times, burning the bamboo was called *bao zhu*. Since the Song Dynasty, people have burned paper-wrapped gunpowder as a substitute. These firecrackers are also called *bao zhang*.

七 賀新年

正月朔望，謂之元旦，俗呼新年。……士夫皆交相賀，細民男女亦皆鮮衣，往來拜節。……不論貧富，游玩琳宮梵宇，竟日不絕。家家宴飲，笑語喧嘩。

宋 吳自牧《夢粱錄》

【語譯】

正月初一，叫作"元旦"，俗稱為"新年"。官吏和讀書人都相互祝賀，普通老百姓家的男女也都穿着漂亮的衣服，你來我往地拜年。不論是窮人還是富人，都去道觀佛寺遊玩，[那兒] 全天 [人流] 不絕。家家都在喝酒吃飯，[到處都是] 響亮的笑聲和說話聲。

【註釋】

1. 賀新年：夏曆新年是中國人最盛大的節日，慶賀新年到來的活動豐富多采，到處都充滿了喜慶吉祥的氣氛。

7 Sending New Year's Greetings[1]

The first day of the first month of the lunar year is called *yuan dan,* or New Year's Day. Officials extend their New Year's greetings to each other. Ordinary people too, don their best clothes and pay New Year's calls. Rich and poor alike visit Buddhist temples and Taoist monasteries in incessant streams throughout the day. Every household enjoys a feast, ringing with conversation and laughter.

Wu Zimu (Song Dynasty):
Records of a Pipe Dream

Notes:

1. Sending New Year's Greetings: The Lunar New Year is the most important festival in China. It is celebrated with a colourful variety of activities in a joyous and auspicious atmosphere.

八　拜年[1]

　　男女依次拜家長畢，主者率卑幼出謁鄰族戚友，或止
遣子弟代賀，謂之拜年。至有歲不相接者，此時亦互相往
拜于門。門首設籍，書姓氏，號為門簿。鮮衣炫路，飛轎
生風。靜巷幽坊，動成鬧市。薄暮至人家者，謂之拜夜
節。

清　顧祿《清嘉錄》

【語譯】

　　[全家] 所有的人按輩份依次禮拜家裏的長輩。之後，[家中]
主要的人領着小輩晚輩去拜訪親戚朋友鄰居等，或只派晚輩前去
代為祝賀，這稱作拜年。終年沒有聯繫的人這時候也相互上門來
拜年。[有些人家] 門口放置的簿冊，[讓來訪者] 書寫姓名的，叫
作門簿。路上鮮亮的衣服令人眩目，腳下生風似的 [轎夫] 使轎子
疾走如飛。[平時] 幽靜的小巷，[此時] 騷動成了鬧市。傍晚到人
家家裏拜訪的，被稱作拜夜節。

【註釋】

1. 拜年：夏曆新年來到時，人們相互上門祝賀新年，稱作拜年。此習俗
　　流傳至今。

8 Paying New Year's Visits[1]

All the younger family members do obeisance to the elders in order of seniority. Then the head of the family leads the juniors in calls on relatives, friends and neighbours, or the juniors are despatched to send greetings on behalf of the family — practices named "paying New Year's visits". Friends never met for the whole year also visit one another at this time. Some households place signature albums called "door books" at the gate to be signed by visitors. People in gaudy clothes look dazzling in the streets, and sedan-chairs move along swiftly like wind. Even quiet lanes now turn into vibrant thoroughfares. Calls made that evening are known as evening courtesy visits.

Gu Lu (Qing Dynasty):
Worthy Records of the Qing Dynasty

Notes:

1. Paying New Year's visits: On the days of Lunar New Year, people visit one another to extend their New Year's wishes. This practice is called "paying a New Year's visit". This custom remains today.

九　新年禁忌

　　元旦為歲朝[1]，比戶懸神軸于中堂，陳設几案，具香燭，祈一歲之安。俗忌掃地、乞火、汲水并針剪。又禁傾穢、瀽糞。忌諱喝粥及湯茶泡飯。天明未起，戒促喚。男子出門必迎喜神方位而行。

清　顧祿《清嘉錄》

【語譯】

　　元旦就是正月初一，家家戶戶在堂屋中掛上神像，擺好長几條案，準備好香和蠟燭，祈求一年的平安。有風俗禁止[這一天]掃地、向別人借火、在井中打水和用針剪。還禁止倒垃圾、倒糞。忌諱喝粥以及吃用茶湯泡的飯。[如果有人]天亮未起牀，絕不能催促他。男人出門必須朝着喜神所在的方向走。

【註釋】

1. 歲朝：夏曆正月初一。

9 New Year's Taboo

Yuan dan is the first day of the year. Every household puts up portraits of divinities in the sitting-room. People set up tables on which joss sticks and candles are lit. Such activities are undertaken to pray for a whole year of peace. According to some customs, activities like sweeping the floor, borrowing fire from others, drawing water and using needles and scissors are taboo. Also, dumping rubbish and manure is prohibited. People abstain from eating porridge or rice soaked in tea. If someone is not up when it is already light, others are not to wake him. If a man goes out, he should walk in the direction of the God of Happiness.

Gu Lu (Qing Dynasty):
Worthy Records of the Qing Dynasty

十 剪紙[1]迎春

立春[2]之日，士大夫家剪紙為小幅，或懸于佳人之首，或綴于花下。

唐　段成式《酉陽雜俎》

立春之日，悉剪彩為燕戴之，帖"宜春"[3]二字。

南朝梁　宗懍《荊楚歲時記》

【語譯】

立春那天，官宦以及讀書人家把小幅的紙張剪 [成小鳥或花的形狀]，有戴在美人頭上的，也有懸掛在花上作點綴的。

立春那天，[人們] 都用五彩的綢剪成燕形，戴在頭上，並 [在門上] 貼上"宜春"二字。

【註釋】

1. 剪紙：古稱"剪彩"，民間稱"剪紙"、"窗花"等。起源很早。大約從西晉起，人們就開始剪紙迎春。此祈吉習俗流行全國。剪紙現已成為中國傳統的手工藝品，有裝飾、欣賞作用。
2. 立春：二十四個節氣之一。中國人以立春為春天的開始。
3. 宜春：稱頌春天的意思。

10 Papercuttings[1] to Welcome Spring

On the first day of Spring[2], the families of officials and scholars cut small pieces of paper [into patterns of birds and flowers], some to be worn on the hair of the beauties, some to be attached to flowers and plants.

Duan Chengshi (Tang Dynasty):
You Yang Records of a Myriad Things

On the first day of Spring people cut patterns of swallows out of colourful silk to be worn on the hair and put characters which mean "pleasant spring" on their doors.

Zong Lin (Southern Dynasties, the State of Liang):
Stories of the Jing and Chu Times

Notes:

1. Papercuttings: sometimes also called floral window decorations, the making of which dates far back to the Western Jin Dynasty (around the 3rd century). At that time, people cut swallow patterns out of colourful silk or paper to celebrate spring. This practice, originally a method of praying for luck, later became popular in all parts of China. Now paper-cutting, is a common, traditional folk art for decorative purpose.

2. the first day of Spring: one of the 24 solar terms, or divisions of the solar year according to the Chinese calendar. The Chinese take this day as the beginning of spring.

十一 鞭春牛

立春候，府縣官吏具公服，禮勾芒[1]，各以彩杖鞭牛者三，勸耕也。

明 劉侗 于奕正《帝京景物略》

立春日，太守集府堂，鞭牛碎之[2]，謂之打春。農民競以麥麻米豆拋打春牛。……百姓買芒神、春牛亭子，置堂中，云宜田事。

清 顧祿《清嘉錄》

【語譯】

立春的時節，府、縣的官員們都穿着禮服，禮拜勾芒神，每人用彩色的棍棒多次鞭打春牛，鼓勵人們耕作。

立春那天，太守匯集在府的廳堂，[用棍棒]把[泥]牛打碎，這稱為打春。農民也爭着把麻、麥子、大米、豆子等拋向春牛。百姓們買勾芒神的像、及[泥作的放在]亭子裏的春牛，[把它們]安置在堂屋中，據説對農事有利。

【註釋】

1. 勾芒：古代傳説中主管農事的神。
2. 鞭牛碎之：春牛是用泥塑成的，通常由當地的行政長官用彩杖將其擊碎。

11 Whipping the Ox in Early Spring

On the first days of the beginning of Spring, officials at the prefecture and the county levels all dress up to worship the god of farming. Afterwards, they whip the ox with decorative rods and sticks, a symbolic gesture to urge tillage.

Liu Tong and Yu Yizheng (Ming Dynasty):
Scenery and Events in the Capital

On the day of the beginning of Spring, officials gather in town halls and shatter a clay ox by whipping it. This practice is called "beating the spring". Farmers vie in sprinkling clay oxen with sesame, barley, rice and bean. Common people buy portraits of the god of farming, and bring clay oxen usually intended for their courtyards into their living rooms because they believe that doing so will be beneficial to husbandry.

Gu Lu (Qing Dynasty):
Worthy Records of the Qing Dynasty

十二　元宵[1]張燈

　　今俗，市上所賣諸燈未改古制，而鄉鎮別邑，又買自郡中，以是元宵前後，喧盛猶昔。……聞最先元夕前後，各採松枝竹葉，結棚于通街，晝則懸彩，雜引流蘇，夜則燃燈，輝煌火樹，衍魚龍，列膏燭，金鼓達旦，名曰燈市，凡闔門[2]以內，大街通路，燈彩遍張，不見天日。

清　顧祿《清嘉錄》

【語譯】

　　現在的習俗，市場上所賣的各種燈都沒有改變古代的樣式，鄉村小鎮、偏僻的小縣 [的人們] 在本地買燈，因此，元宵節前後，熱鬧的情景還如往昔一樣。聽說最早元宵節前後，[人們] 採了松樹枝和竹葉，在大路上搭起棚，白天掛着彩綢，中間垂蕩着 [絲線編的] 穗子，夜裏點起了燈。燈樹燦爛輝煌。[人們把彩燈] 變幻出魚、龍的樣子，豎起 [燃燒着的] 蠟燭，敲擊金屬的樂器和鼓直到天亮，這叫"燈市"。城門以內所有的大街小巷到處都佈置着燈彩，遮住了天空和太陽。

12   The Lantern Festival[1]

According to the present practices, the lanterns sold in the cities nowadays have not changed much from the ancient types. People in towns and remote counties still buy their local makes. Therefore, on the days around the Lantern Festival, the scene is just as exhilarating as it was in old times. It is said that in ancient times people gathered pine boughs and bamboo leaves to put up sheds in the main streets on the days around the Lantern Festival. During the daytime, colourful silks were hung with tassels dangling in their midst. When night fell, lanterns were lit. Trees of lanterns created a luminous and resplendent scene. The lanterns shone in patterns of fish and dragons. Huge candles were lit, and drums and gongs were heard everywhere until daybreak. This celebration was called the Lantern Fair. Colourful lanterns adorned the streets and lanes within the city walls. They even eclipsed the sun and the sky.

Gu Lu (Qing Dynasty):
Worthy Records of the Qing Dynasty

【註釋】

1. 元宵：夏曆正月十五日是元宵節，中國人生活中重大而熱烈的傳統節日。流行於全國各地。除了張燈、觀燈外，還有猜燈謎、走百病以及擊太平鼓、舞龍等民間文藝活動。飲食方面習慣於吃元宵（湯圓）、年糕、餃子等，以示家人團聚，生活美滿。

2. 閶門：在蘇州市城西，唐代時十分繁榮的地方。

Notes:

1. The Lantern Festival: It falls on January 15th of the lunar year. For the Chinese, it is an important and happy traditional holiday. This holiday originated in the Han Dynasty and is now popularly celebrated in all parts of the country. Apart from putting up and appreciating the lanterns, activities such as solving lantern riddles, walking long distances to drive away all diseases, beating the peace drum and performing the dragon dance are also included. People eat sweet dumplings made from glutinous rice flour, New Year's cake, and salty dumplings to signify family reunion and joyful living.

十三 清明節¹

　　三月清明日，男女掃墓，擔提尊榼，轎馬後掛楮錠²，
粲粲然滿道也。拜者、酹者、哭者、為墓除草添土者，焚
楮錠次，以紙錢³置墳頭……哭罷，不歸也，趨芳草，擇
園圃，列坐盡醉。有歌者、哭笑無端，哀往而樂回也。是
日簪柳，游高粱橋⁴，曰踏青，多四方客未歸者，祭掃日感
念出游。

明　劉侗　于奕正《帝京景物略》

【語譯】

　　[夏曆] 三月清明節，[民間] 男女去掃墓。[人們] 挑着或提着
酒器食盒，轎子、車馬後掛着紙錠，熙熙攘攘，路上滿是人。[墓
地裏]有的人在跪拜，有的人把酒灑在地上祭奠，有的人在哭，有
的人在除去墳上的雜草並添上新土。[人們] 在焚燒紙錠的同時，
又將紙錢放在墳頭上。……[他們] 哭完不 [馬上] 回去，而是趕
着去一個有花草樹木的地方，選擇一片綠地，一個個坐着直至一
醉方休。有個唱歌的人，無緣無故地時哭時笑，這真是傷心地來
快活地去啊！這一天，人們還在鬢際上插楊柳，[在郊外的] 高粱
橋遊玩，這叫"踏青"。大多數來自四方而沒有回家的人，是那些
在祭掃 [親人的] 日子裏思想着出去遊樂的人。

13   The Clear Brightness Festival[1]

On a day in the third month of the lunar year (usually April 5 by the solar calendar), people sweep their ancestral tombs. They bring wine and food in baskets or on bamboo poles resting on their shoulders. Some travel on sedan chairs or in carriages aglitter with strings of paper ingots[2], on roads crowded with people. They kowtow and pour libations at the tombs. Then they weed and add fresh soil to the tombs. Afterwards, they burn the strings of paper ingots and place coin-shaped pieces of paper on top of the graves as an offering to the dead. After weeping, instead of leaving, they find a pleasant place with trees and flowers to sit down and drink to their hearts' content. Some sing, laugh or cry for no reason. Though they go out sad, they return happy. On this day, people wear willows in their hair and visit the Sorghum Bridge[3]. This custom is called "walking on the green"[4]. From far and near, many come and do not think of going home early because they make this excuse to enjoy an outing.

Liu Tong and Yu Yizheng (Ming Dynasty):
Scenery and Events in the Capital

【註釋】

1. 清明節：時間在夏曆三月，公曆四月五日左右。中國人重要的傳統節日。古代清明前一天是寒食節，由於兩節時間相近，現已融合成一個節日。此日民間有掃墓、踏青、插柳、吃青糰等習俗。

2. 楮錠：紙錠。用錫箔糊製成的銀錠狀的冥錢。

3. 紙錢：紙錢有圓形方孔的，也有在紙上打上錢印的。與紙錠不同處在於不予焚燒，祭掃結束時置於墳頭。當代喪葬習俗則將其焚燒。

4. 高粱橋：在北京西城外。

Notes:

1. The Clear Brightness Festival: usually falls on April 5th of the solar calendar. It is a time for people to visit and clean their ancestral tombs, to make excursions in the countryside, to put on willow branches and eat dumplings specially made for the occasion.

2. paper ingots: joss paper made of tinfoil and paper, folded in the shape of ingots, the burning of which is believed to transmit wealth to one's ancestors.

3. Sorghum Bridge: located in the western suburb of Beijing, known for its beautiful scenery.

4. walking on the green: the practice of taking excursions in the countryside in spring when the hills and plains are green.

十四　端午節[1]划船比賽

是日，競渡[2]，採雜藥。

按：五月五日競渡，俗為屈原[3]投汨羅日，傷其死，故并命舟楫以拯之。舸舟取其輕利謂之飛鳧，一自以為水軍[4]，一自以為水馬。州將及士人悉臨水而觀之。

南朝梁　宗懍《荊楚歲時記》

【語譯】

[夏曆五月初五] 這一天，舉行划船比賽，採集各種各樣的草藥。

按語：五月五日划船比賽，這風俗是因為屈原在這一天投汨羅江 [而死]，人們哀憐他的死，所以都用船去救他。賽船用輕快便利的那種，人們稱它為飛鳧。[比賽雙方] 一邊自稱為"水上兵車"，另一邊自稱為"水上駿馬"。州郡的官長和有身份的人都去水邊觀看。

14 The Dragon Boat Festival[1]

On the fifth day of the fifth month of the lunar year a boat race is held and people gather all kinds of herbal medicines.

The explanation is this: the boat race on the fifth day of the fifth lunar month is undertaken to commemorate the poet Qu Yuan[2] who drowned himself in the Mi Luo River that day. People sympathize with his death. Therefore they row boats to come to his rescue symbolically. The competitors use light, swift boats which are called "flying wild ducks". The two teams in the rowing competition call themselves "Chariot on Water" and "Steed on Water". Prefecture officials and people of prestige all go to the riverside to watch the performance.

Zong Lin (Southern Dynasties, the State of Liang):
Stories of the Jing and Chu Times

【註釋】

1. 端午節：在夏曆五月初五，是流行於全國的傳統大節。這天民間有賽龍舟、吃粽子、飲雄黃酒、掛香囊、插菖蒲和採草藥等習俗。

2. 競渡：划船比賽。多採用龍船來進行比賽，故也稱為"賽龍舟"。

3. 屈原：戰國時代楚國人，偉大的愛國詩人。被楚國國君放逐到湘江一帶，後因深感楚國政治腐敗，自己無力挽救，投汨羅江而死。

4. 水軍：指水車，故稱水上兵車。

Notes:

1. The Dragon Boat Festival: It falls on May 5th of the lunar year. This is a major festival celebrated all over the country. Activities include dragon-boat races, eating rice dumplings (See Passage 15), drinking yellow wine, wearing incense sachets, putting up bunches of sweet flag and gathering herbal medicines.

2. Qu Yuan: a patriotic poet, citizen of the State of Chu during the Warring States Period (5th century B.C.). He was exiled to the Xiang River by the Emperor. Greatly concerned over the corruption in the government and feeling powerless to remedy it, he drowned himself in the Mi Luo River.

十五　端午節吃粽子 [1]

　　粽俗作糉。古人以菰蘆葉裹黍米煮成，尖角，如棕櫚葉心之形，故曰粽，曰角黍，近世多用糯米矣。今俗五月五日以為節物，相餽送，或言為祭屈原 [2] 作此投江，以飼蛟龍也。

　　　　　　　　　　　　　　明　李時珍《本草綱目》

【語譯】

　　"粽"通常寫作"糉"。古代人們用菰蘆的葉子裹着黃米煮熟，[外形上有] 尖尖的角，像棕櫚樹的葉心的形狀，所以稱它"粽子"，或叫"角黍"。近代大多用糯米做了。現代的習俗 [把粽子] 作為應節的物品，相互贈送，有人說是為了祭祀屈原，做粽子投到江中，用它來餵蛟龍的。

【註釋】

1. 粽子：端午節的節日傳統食品，至今流行全國。傳說古人將粽子投入江中餵蛟龍，以免它吃去屈原的屍體。
2. 屈原：參見前篇"端午節划船比賽"。

15　Eating Rice Dumplings[1] in the Dragon Boat Festival

In ancient times rice dumplings were made from broomcorn millet wrapped in gourd leaves. They had a horn shape like the heart of a palm leaf and were therefore called *zong* in Chinese, or sometimes, horned broomcorn. In modern times, these dumplings are made from glutinous rice. Now it is customary to exchange rice dumplings as a festival gift. Some say the *zong* are made as sacrifices to Qu Yuan[2]. People in the past made these dumplings and cast them into the water to feed the dragon.

Li Shizhen (Ming Dynasty):
A Compendium of Materia Medica

Notes:

1. rice dumplings: a traditional food eaten on Dragon Boat Festival Day, now commonly eaten all over China. Legends have it that people in the past threw these dumplings into the water to feed the dragon that haunted the river so that it would not eat the body of Qu Yuan.

2. Qu Yuan: Please refer to notes on Dragon Boat Festival (Passage 14).

十六 端午節驅五毒[1]

　　尼庵剪五色彩箋，狀蟾蜍、蜥蜴、蜘蛛、蛇、蚖之形，分貽檀越，貼門楣寢次，能魘毒蟲，謂之五毒符。……案：《青齊風俗記》："谷雨[2]日，畫五毒符，圖蝎子、蜈蚣、虺蛇、蜂、蜮之狀，各畫一針刺之，刊布家戶，以禳蟲毒。"吳俗，則在端五。

清　顧祿《清嘉錄》

【語譯】

　　尼姑庵的女尼，用彩色的薄綢剪出蟾蜍、蜥蜴、蜘蛛、蛇和多足蟲的形狀，分送給施主們，[讓他們在端午節時]貼在門楣和臥室中，[據說]能鎮住毒蟲，這叫"五毒符"。按語：《青齊風俗記》說："谷雨那天，畫五毒符，畫上蝎子、蜈蚣、毒蛇、黃蜂和蜮的樣子，並在每一樣上畫一根針刺著它們，刻印後，佈置在人家的門戶上，用來祈求趕走各種蟲類毒疫。"吳地的習俗，是在端午時[佈置五毒符的]。

16 Driving Away the Five Poisonous Pests[1]

Nuns in Buddhist nunneries cut out of colourful thin silk patterns of toads, lizards, spiders, snakes and centipedes and distribute them to their benefactors to be posted on doors and in bedrooms before the Dragon Boat Festival. It is believed that the cutouts can suppress such poisonous vermin. These emblems are thus called the "amulets against the five poisonous pests". According to The Customs of Qingqi, on Grain Rain Day[2] people painted "amulets against the five poisonous pests" in the shapes of the lizard, the centipede, the poisonous snake, the wasp and the demon, each impaled by a needle. These paintings were duplicated and put up on the doors of the houses in an attempt to drive away all pests and pestilences. In the Wu area this custom is practised during the Dragon Boat Festival.

> Gu Lu (Qing Dynasty):
> *Worthy Records of the Qing Dynasty*

【註釋】

1. 驅五毒：流行於全中國的端午習俗。俗傳，毒蟲都在端午起開始孳生，因此必須在端午時貼五毒符。此外，還在屋角噴雄黃酒、灑石灰、燃藥煙以殺毒蟲，除穢氣。

2. 谷雨：二十四節氣之一，在四月二十日左右。

Notes:

1. Driving away the five poisonous pests: This is a tradition observed all over the country in the Dragon Boat Festival. It is a popular belief that poisonous vermin start to multiply on the day of the Dragon Boat Festival. Therefore people put up "amulets against the five poisonous pests" before that day. In addition, realgar wine is sprayed and lime powder is sprinkled in the corners of the houses. Herbs are burnt to kill the five poisonous pests and drive away malignities.

2. Grain Rain Day: the sixth of the 24 solar terms, which usually falls around April 20 of the lunar year.

十七　乞巧節[1]

　　七月七日為牽牛織女[2]聚會之夜。是夕，人家婦女結
彩縷，穿七孔針[3]，或以金銀鍮石[4]為針，陳瓜果于庭以乞
巧，有喜子[5]網于瓜上，則以為應符。

南朝梁　宗懍《荊楚歲時記》

【語譯】

　　[夏曆] 七月初七之夜是 [傳說中] 牛郎織女在銀河相會的時
候。這天晚上，民間婦女用彩色的綫編結，並穿帶有七個孔眼的
針，或穿用金、銀、黃銅製的針。[婦女們] 在庭院裏擺上瓜果 [等
供物向織女] 乞求智巧。[如果發現] 有蜘蛛在瓜果上結起了網，
就被認為是 [得到了] 應答 [的吉兆]。

17　The Double Seventh Festival[1]

The seventh day of the seventh month of the lunar year is the day when the legendary Cowherd and the Girl Weaver[2] meet in the Milky Way. On that night, women crochet with colourful silk threads. They pull threads through seven-holed comb-like needles, or needles made of gold, silver or copper. They place fruits and melons in their yards, offerings for which they hope the Girl Weaver will reward them with skill in needlework. They are happy if they find webs woven by spiders on the fruit because they think this is a good omen and that the Girl Weaver has agreed to fulfil their wishes.

Zong Lin (Southern Dynasties, the State of Liang):
<u>Stories of the Jing and Chu Times</u>

【註釋】

1. 乞巧節：也稱"七夕"、"女節"、"少女節"、"雙七節"。作為古代婦女的節日，這天的活動都圍繞着婦女或女孩求智乞巧展開。

2. 牽牛織女：傳說織女是天帝的孫女，心靈手巧，能織造精美的服裝。後嫁給河西牽牛，婚後不再織造。天帝大怒，責令兩人分離，織女仍回河東生活，每年七月初七才准他們相見一次。

3. 七孔針：形狀如篦子，有七個孔，專為乞巧用，不能用於縫紉。

4. 鍮石：即黃銅。

5. 喜子：指一種身體細長，常在宅內結網的蜘蛛。由於它的結網被認為是吉兆，故稱它為"喜子"或"喜蛛"。

Notes:

1. The Double Seventh Festival: also named "maiden's day", "daughter's day", was a festival for women in ancient China. The ceremonies on that day were held for the purpose of seeking dexterity for girls and married women.

2. the Cowherd and the Girl Weaver: In Chinese legend, the Girl Weaver was the Jade Emperor's grand-daughter. She was clever and deft, and good at tailoring. After marrying the Cowherd on the west bank of the Heavenly River (the Milky Way), she stopped sewing. This enraged the Jade Emperor greatly. He ordered them to separate. The Girl Weaver was sent back to the east bank of the river. They were allowed to meet only once a year on July 7 of the lunar calendar. The Girl Weaver is equivalent to the Vega and the Cowherd is equivalent to the Altair.

十八 放河燈[1]

　　至中元日例有盂蘭會[2]，扮演秧歌、獅子[3]諸雜技。晚間沿河燃燈，謂之放河燈。

清　富察敦崇《燕京歲時記》

　　選僧為瑜珈焰口，造盂蘭盆[4]，放荷花燈，中夜開船，張燈如元夕，謂之盂蘭盆會。蓋江南中元節，每多婦女買舟作盂蘭放焰口，燃燈水面，以賭勝負，秦淮最勝。

清　李斗《揚州畫舫錄》

【語譯】

　　到 [夏曆七月十五日] 中元節照例有盂蘭盆會，有扭秧歌、舞獅子等各種雜技表演。晚上人們把點燃了的燈沿河放入水中，稱為放河燈。

　　選了和尚來唸焰口經，[為了施食餓鬼和超度亡靈]。作盂蘭盆，放荷花燈，半夜開船，到處掛着燈如元宵節一樣，這稱為"盂蘭盆會"。每逢江南中元節時，很多婦女租船、燒盂蘭盆、找和尚唸焰口經，在水面上點燃了燈 [進行比賽]，賭勝與負，這時，秦淮河上最熱鬧。

18 Floating River Lanterns[1]

As a rule, there is a Yulan Pot Fair[2] on the day of the Zhong Yuan Festival. People put on performances such as the *yang ge* dance, the lion dance[3] and other acrobatic shows. When evening comes, people float lit lanterns along the rivers. This practice is called "floating river lanterns".

Fucha Duncong (Qing Dynasty):
Annual Records of the Capital

Special monks are invited to chant Buddhist fire scriptures, the purpose of which is to feed hungry ghosts and release souls from purgatory. People make *yulan* pots, float lotus lamps and go boating at midnight. Lanterns are hung everywhere just as on Lantern Festival Day. This occasion is named Yulan Pot Fair. In the areas south of the Yangtze River in the Zhong Yuan Festival, women rent boats, burn *yulan* pots and employ monks to chant Buddhist fire scriptures. They also compete in lighting up lamps and floating them on the river and betting on the outcome. The Qinhuai River witnesses the most jubilant festivity.

Li Dou (Qing Dynasty):
Records in a Gaily-Painted Pleasure Boat in Yangzhou

【註釋】

1. 放河燈：夏曆七月十五晚上，人們把燈放入水中，燈內燃燭，放在水面上任其漂流。相傳可為陰間的鬼魂引路。燈的形狀各異，多數是蓮花燈。

2. 盂蘭會：又稱"盂蘭盆會"參見第五十一篇"中元節祭祀亡靈"一則。

3. 秧歌獅子：最為常見的兩項民間藝術表演。扭秧歌時，舞者穿彩服，隨着鑼鼓點扭演蹦跳，北方特別盛行。舞獅者藏身在紋有彩色圖案的假獅身中，模仿獅子的動作，表演極為生動活潑。

4. 盂蘭盆：參見第五十一篇"中元節祭祀亡靈"一則。

Notes:

1. Floating river lanterns: On the evening of July 15 of the lunar year, people float candlelit lanterns on the river. It is believed that the lanterns can illuminate the way out for ghosts and spirits in the nether world. The lanterns are made in different shapes, but most of them are in the shape of the lotus, which signifies the release of the souls of the dead from purgatory.

2. Yu Lan Pot Fair: See Passage 51 "Zhong Yuan Festival".

3. *yang ge* dance and lion dance: Two of the most popular folk dance performances. In doing the *yang ge* dance, dancers are dressed in colourful costumes and strut vivaciously to the rhythm of the drums. This kind of dance is most popular in the northern part of China. Lion dance performers dress themselves in lion costumes and mimic lion movements, a vivid and lively performance.

十九　中秋¹賞月

　　八月十五中秋節……王孫公子，富家巨室，莫不登危樓，臨軒玩月……至如鋪席之家，亦登小小月臺，安排家宴，團圓子女，以酬佳節。雖陋巷貧樓之人，解衣市酒，勉強迎歡，不肯虛度。此夜天街買賣，直至五鼓，玩月游人，婆娑于市，至曉不絕。

宋　吳自牧《夢粱錄》

【語譯】

　　八月十五是中秋節，王孫公子 [這些有地位的人] 以及富豪之家，一個個都登上高樓，靠着窗檻賞月。至於像開店鋪這樣的人家，也登上小小的露天平台，擺上家宴，和子女們團圓，歡度佳節。即使是狹陋街巷中貧窮 [不堪] 的人，也脫下衣服換酒喝，竭盡全力歡慶，不肯馬馬虎虎過節。這夜，京城街市上的生意一直做到五更時分，賞月的人在市上悠遊徘徊，直到天亮仍然不斷。

【註釋】

1. 中秋：中秋節是中國人的傳統大節，時間在夏曆八月十五日。民間以合家團圓為主要內容，此外還包括吃月餅、舞龍燈等活動。

19 Admiring the Full Moon during the Mid-Autumn Festival[1]

The fifteenth day of the eighth lunar month is the Mid-Autumn Festival. On this night, people of prestige and wealth climb to the top of tall buildings. There, leaning on the railings, they admire the moon. Lesser business people also go up to small open balconies. They arrange family feasts and spend the holiday with their children. Even poor people in the narrow alleys trade their clothes for wine. They try their best to celebrate this holiday in order not to let it pass in vain. On this night, the commotion in the streets of the capital lasts until the fifth watch of the night. People admiring the moon pace up and down the market till daybreak.

Wu Zimu (Song Dynasty):
Records of a Pipe Dream

Notes:

1. Mid-Autumn Festival: a major traditional Chinese festival which is widely celebrated in all parts of the country. People admire the moon in families. They also eat moon cakes and enjoy the illunimated dragon dance.

二十　中秋拜月[1]

　　傾城人家子女，不以貧富，自能行至十二三，皆以成人之服飾之，登樓或于中庭焚香拜月，各有所期。

宋　金盈之《新編醉翁談錄》

　　比戶瓶花香蠟，望空頂禮，小兒女膜拜月下，嬉戲燈前，謂之齋月宮。

清　顧祿《清嘉錄》

【語譯】

　　全城所有家庭的孩子，不論是有錢的，還是沒錢的，從能自己走路到十二三歲的，都用成人的服飾打扮他們，[讓他們] 登上樓，或在院子裏焚起香祭拜月神，每個孩子都有自己的願望。

　　家家戶戶都把花插在瓶裏，[安放好] 香和蠟燭，眼望着天空跪拜，小孩子跪在地上，舉兩手虔誠地行禮，又在燈前遊戲玩耍，這稱為祭月神。

【註釋】

1.　拜月：亦稱"祭月"、"禮月"。中秋節夜在庭院中禮拜月神的活動，流行於全國大多數地區。北方祭月時，供品中還有月兔像。

56

20　Worshipping the Moon[1] during the Mid-Autumn Festival

All the children in town, rich or poor, from toddlers to teens, are dressed up in adults' clothes. They either go up on the roofs or gather in the yards to burn joss sticks and pray to the moon, each with his or her own wishes.

Jin Yingzhi (Song Dynasty):
New Edition of the Babblings of a Drunkard

Every household in town arranges flowers in vases, lights joss sticks and candles and directs prayers skywards. Kids kneel, and raising their hands, they bow ardently to the moon. Afterwards they play in the lamplight. This activity is called "worshipping the Moon God".

Gu Lu (Qing Dynasty):
Worthy Records of the Qing Dynasty

Notes:

1. Worshipping the moon: People offer prayers and sacrifices to the moon in the Mid-Autumn Festival. This custom is observed in most parts of China. In the north, people include a portrait of the Moon Rabbit in the offerings.

二十一　重陽節 [1]

　　九月九日，載酒具、茶罏、食榼，曰登高 [2]。香山諸山，高山也；法藏寺，高塔也；靈顯宮、報國寺，高閣也，釋不登。賃園亭，闖坊曲 [3]，為娛耳。麵餅種棗栗其面，星星然，曰花糕 [4]。糕肆標綵旗，曰花糕旗。父母家必迎女來食花糕，或不得迎，母則詬，女則怨詫，小妹則泣，望其姐姨，亦曰女兒節。

明　劉侗　于奕正《帝京景物略》

【語譯】

　　[夏曆] 九月初九，[人們] 帶着酒具、茶壺、食盒登高去。香山 [一帶] 各山都是高山；法藏寺有高塔，靈顯寺、報國寺有高閣。僧人是不登高的。[人們] 租了園子亭子，闖沖沖去娛樂場所，是為了玩樂一下。棗子、栗子就像 [密佈的] 星星那樣點綴着麵粉作的花糕。糕店還在上面插了一面面的彩色紙旗，人稱"花糕旗"。[這一天] 父母一定要迎接出嫁的女兒歸來共食花糕。有的沒有迎到，作母親的就要責備，作女兒的 [也滿懷] 怨尤和詫異，年幼的妹妹則要哭泣，盼望她的姐姐 [回來]，[所以這一天] 也稱為"女兒節"。

58

21 The Chong Yang Festival[1]

On the ninth day of the ninth lunar month, people take wine glasses, teapots and food boxes and go up the mountains[2]. All the mountains in the Xiangshan range are high. In these mountains are Fazang Temple with a tall pagoda; Xianling Temple and Baoguo Temple, both elevated structures. Monks do not go up the mountains, but common people rent mountain gardens and pavilions or go to the pleasure haunts[3] in the mountains to have fun.

The pastry shops sell cakes sprinkled with dates and chestnuts as thick as stars in a night sky. These cakes are called *hua gao*[4] — flower cakes. Pastry shop owners usually put colourful paper flags on their cakes. The flags are called "flower cake flags". On that day, parents expect their married daughters to return home to eat the flower cakes. If the daughter cannot come, the mother will complain, the daughter will be filled with sadness, and the younger sister will weep because she really wants to enjoy this rare chance to see her sister. Thus, this day is also called Daughter's Day.

Liu Tong, Yu Yizheng (Ming Dynasty):
Scenery and Events in the Capital

【註釋】

1. 重陽節：夏曆九月初九重陽節，是流行全國的傳統節日。古人認為九是陽數(單數)，九月九正好是兩個陽數相重，故稱重陽節。這天，民間有登高野遊、賞菊喝酒、吃花糕，迎出嫁女等活動。

2. 登高：據說東漢人桓景拜仙人費長房為師。費長房對他說，某年九月初九有大災，但如將茱萸(一種植物)繫在手臂上，登山飲菊花酒，此禍可消除。桓景照他所說，全家登山，果然平安無事。傍晚回到家中，發現雞犬牛羊全死去了。從此，每年九月初九，人們都登山野餐、佩帶茱萸，飲菊花酒，以求避禍呈祥。

3. 坊曲：妓女所居之地。有錢人常借坊曲作為宴飲、娛樂、交易等的場所。

4. 花糕：也叫重陽糕。吃糕的原因是因為"糕"與"登高"的"高"同音。

Notes:

1. Chong Yang Festival: September 9 of the lunar year is the Chong Yang Festival. In ancient China, odd numbers were regarded as positive numbers. September 9 (9/9) contains two positive numbers. Thus the day is named *"chong yang"*, or double positive. On this day, common people hold activities such as going up the mountains, having an outing, admiring chrysanthemums, drinking wine, eating flower cakes and welcoming back married daughters.

2. go up the mountains: It is said a man in the Eastern Han Dynasty named Huan Jing acknowledged the immortal Fei Chang Fang as his teacher. One day, Fei warned Huan Jing that there would be a major disaster on September 9 in a certain year. But if he wore cornel leaves around his arm, climbed a mountain and drank chrysanthemum wine, the disaster could be averted. Huan Jing did accordingly. He took his family up a mountain and all was well. When he returned home in the evening, he found all his livestock had died mysteriously. Thereafter, on September 9 people climb the mountains and have picnics. They also wear cornel leaves and drink chrysanthemum wine to avoid misfortune and seek good luck.

3. pleasure haunts: Here they refer to brothels. Rich people rented brothels as places for banquets, gatherings and business.

4. *hua gao*: It is also called *"chong yang gao"*. The reason for eating *hua gao* is because the word *"gao (cake)"* in Chinese is homonymous with the word *"gao* (high, i.e. high mountain)".

二十二　冬至大如年[1]

　　郡人最重冬至節，先日，親朋各以食物相饋送，提筐
擔盒，充斥道路，俗呼冬至盤。節前一夕，俗呼冬至夜。
是夜，人家更速燕飲，謂之節酒。女嫁而歸寧在室者，至
是，必歸壻家。家無大小，必市食物以享先，間有懸掛祖
先遺容者。諸凡儀文，加于常節，故有“冬至大如年”之
諺。

清　顧祿《清嘉錄》

【語譯】

　　郡中的人最重視冬至節，[節前]早幾天，親戚朋友相互饋贈
食品，路上擠滿了提着筐挑着盒子的人，俗稱這為“冬至盤”。冬
至節前一夜，俗稱為“冬至夜”。這夜家家輪流請人來吃飯喝酒，
這稱為“節酒”。已出嫁的婦女在娘家的，在這天一定回丈夫家
去。無論是大戶人家還是小戶人家，必定要買食品祭祀祖先，其
中也有懸掛祖先遺像的人家。所有各種儀式規定都比普通的節日
隆重，因此有“冬至大如年”這樣的俗諺。

22 The Winter Solstice[1]

People in the prefectures attach great importance to the Winter Solstice. Several days previously, friends and relatives present gifts of food to one another. The streets are crowded with people carrying baskets and boxes which are generally called "winter solstice trays". The night before is called Winter Solstice Eve. On that night, families invite guests to food and drinks. This dinner is called the festival banquet. Married women who happen to be staying with their parents must return to their husbands. Families, rich and poor alike, buy food to offer to their ancestors. Some put up the portraits of their ancestors. The ceremonies and customs are more splendid than those of the ordinary festivals. Therefore, the saying goes, "The Winter Solstice is as important as the New Year".

Gu Lu (Qing Dynasty):
Worthy Records of the Qing Dynasty

【註釋】

1. 冬至大如年：冬至，是農曆二十四個節氣之一，在公曆十二月二十二日左右，這天北半球黑夜最長，白天最短。民間稱冬至節為"過小年"，有的地區認為此節的隆重程度與過新年一樣，所以説"冬至大如年"。甚至還有"肥冬瘦年"的説法，由此可見民間對冬至節的重視了。

Notes:

1. The Winter Solstice: one of the twenty-four solar terms. It is around 22nd December of the solar year. On that day in the northern hemisphere, the night is the longest and the day the shortest in the whole year. The Winter Solstice is popularly called the "small New Year". In some areas people think the Winter Solstice should be celebrated as grandly as the New Year. Thus, the saying goes, "Fat Winter Solstice and lean New Year". This shows the importance people attach to the Winter Solstice.

二十三　送竈神¹

廿四日，以糖劑餅²、黍糕、棗栗、胡桃、炒豆祀竈
君，以槽草秣竈君馬，謂竈君翌日朝天去，白家間一歲事。
祝曰：“好多說，不好少說。”……今男祭，禁不令婦女
見之。

明　劉侗　于奕正《帝京景物略》

【語譯】

[夏曆臘月]二十四日，[人們]用小糖餅、黃米糕、棗子、栗
子、胡桃、炒豆祭祀竈神，用餵牲口的草料餵竈的馬。傳說竈神
翌日要上天去報告家中一年內的事。[人們對着竈神]禱告：“好的
事情請多報告一些，不好的事情請少說一些。”……現在都由男人
祭竈，有禁忌不讓女人看祭祀的情形。

66

23 Seeing the Kitchen God Off [1]

On 24th of the last month in the lunar calendar, families worship the Kitchen God with offerings of homemade candies[2], rice cakes, dates, walnuts and fried beans. They also burn fodder as a gesture symbolic of feeding the Kitchen God's horse. It is believed that the Kitchen God will return to heaven the next day and report on the deeds of each family during the previous year to the Jade Emperor. So they pray to the Kitchen God: "Speak more of the virtues of the family and less of its evil deeds." ... The ceremonial part of this celebration is presided over by a man, and, according to a taboo, women are not allowed to view the ceremonies.

Liu Tong and Yu Yizheng (Ming Dynasty):
Scenery and Events in the Capital

【註釋】

1. 竈神：傳說中掌管一家禍福的神靈。它的神龕置於廚房大竈的上方。民間通常在夏曆十二月二十四日祭竈神。祭祀後即焚去舊神像換上新神像。

2. 糖劑餅：也叫"竈糖"。一種用麥芽糖製成的土糖，祭竈時必備。據說目的為了甜住竈神的心，盼它在天帝前多說好話。同時也為了黏住它的嘴，使它不能搬弄是非。

Notes:

1. Kitchen God: It is said that the Kitchen God is in control of a family's fortunes and misfortunes. His shrine is located above the kitchen stove. He reports the good and evil people did on earth to the Jade Emperor on the 23rd or 24th of December of the lunar year. Ordinary families usually offer sacrifices to the Kitchen God that day. At the end of the ceremony the old portrait of the Kitchen God is burnt and a new one is put up.

2. homemade candies: Offerings including candies made from malt sugar are intended to please the Kitchen God so that he will only talk about the good deeds of a family. People also hope that the sticky sweets will seal the Kitchen God's mouth so that he will tell no tales.

二十四　娃娃親[1]

　　燕趙[2]之間，居民家道之小康者，生子三五齡，輒為娶及笄之女。家貧子多者，輒利其聘貲，從俗遣嫁焉。女至男家，先以父母禮見翁姑，以弟呼其婿，一切井臼、烹調、縫紉之事，悉皆任之。夜者撫婿而眠，晝者為之着衣，為之飼食，如媬姆然。子長成，乃合巹[3]。

徐珂《清稗類鈔》

【語譯】

　　燕、趙這一帶地方的居民，家庭情況屬於小康水平的，生了兒子才三歲五歲，就給他娶個成年的姑娘。家庭貧寒孩子又多的人家，則 [認為] 他們的聘金有利可圖，就隨當地的風俗習慣讓 [女孩] 出嫁。姑娘到了男方家，先用對父母的禮儀拜見公婆，稱她的丈夫為弟弟。[家中] 所有打水舂米、煮飯燒菜和縫紉等 [家務]，全部由她來擔任。晚上哄 [小] 女婿睡覺，白天給他穿衣服，餵飯給他吃，像媬姆那樣。男孩子成年後，便結婚。

24   Infant Matrimony[1]

In the states of Yan and Zhao[2], the son of a relatively well-off family would be betrothed to a grown-up girl when he was between the ages of three and five. Anticipating that their daughters' betrothal gifts would be profitable, poor families with a lot of children would marry them in accordance with the local custom. When the betrothed girl arrived at the in-laws, the first thing she did was to make obeisance to her parents-in-law in the way she did to her own parents, and she addressed her husband as "younger brother". Chores like fetching water from a well, grinding rice in a mortar, cooking and sewing all fell on her. At night, she would lull her little husband to sleep; during the daytime, she dressed him and fed him. She actually served as a maid in the house. They married when the boy grew up.

Xu Ke: <u>Classified Anecdotes of the Qing Dynasty</u>

【註釋】

1. 娃娃親：即是為尚處在幼年的兒子娶媳婦。舊時流行在許多地區的一種婚俗。

2. 燕趙：指河北省一帶。

3. 合卺：指成婚。

Notes:

1. Infant matrimony: i.e., to marry a young girl to an infant boy. In ancient times it was a custom popular in many parts of China.

2. the states of Yan and Zhao: ancient states in the present-day Hebei Province.

二十五 下財禮[1]

　　且論聘禮，富貴之家當備三金送之，則金釧，金鐲、金帔墜者是也。若鋪席宅舍，或無金器，以銀鍍代之，否則貧富不同，亦從其便，此無定法耳。更言士宦，亦送銷金大袖，黃羅銷金裙，段紅長裙，或紅素羅大繡段亦得。……又送官會[2]銀錠，謂之“下財禮”。

宋　吳自牧《夢粱錄》

【語譯】

　　談到聘禮，有錢有地位的人家應該準備“三金”送給女方，那就是金臂鐲、金手鐲和金的披肩裝飾品。如果是開店鋪的人家，有的沒有金器，就用鍍銀的代替，反正窮人和富人是不同的，也是根據每家的經濟能力 [決定] 的，這並沒 [硬性] 規定。再說官宦 [人家]，還送嵌金線的大袖衣、黃羅緞嵌金線的裙子、紅色的緞子長裙，或者 [送] 紅羅緞上繡大幅 [圖案] 的衣料也可以。又送紙幣和銀錠，這些就叫作“下財禮”。

【註釋】

1. 下財禮：也稱“下聘禮”。指在完婚前，男家向女家送財禮。流行於全國大部分地區的婚俗。
2. 官會：宋代發行的一種紙幣。

25   Betrothal Gifts[1]

Talking about betrothal gifts, rich and powerful families prepare "three golds" to offer to the girl's family — a gold armlet, a gold bracelet and a cape with gold decorations. Small business families which do not possess any gold articles, use silver-plated articles as a substitute. At any rate, there is a difference between the rich and the poor. It all depends on their financial ability and there is no rule about this. In addition to those things mentioned above, families of government officials will also send these gifts: a wide-sleeved overcoat, a long yellow silk skirt, both embroidered with gold thread; and a red silk dress, or a piece of red silk cloth with large embroidered patterns. They also send paper money and silver ingots. All these are betrothal gifts.

Wu Zimu (Song Dynasty):
Records of a Pipe Dream

Notes:

1. betrothal gifts: These are the gifts that the young man's family should send to the girl's family before marriage. This is a marital custom observed in most parts of China.

二十六　新娘蒙首[1]

　　近時娶婦，以紅帕蒙首。按《通典》杜佑曰：“自東漢魏晉以來，時或艱處，歲遇吉，急於嫁娶，乃以紗縠蒙女首，而夫氏發之。因拜舅姑，便成婚禮，六禮[2]悉舍。”合巹[3]復棄，是蒙首之法，亦相傳已久。但古或以失時急娶之用，今則為通行之禮耳。

清　趙翼《陔餘叢考》

【語譯】

　　近代人娶新娘，用紅色的手帕蒙住她的頭。按《通典》的作者杜佑說法是，自東漢、魏晉以來，時時有艱難憂患的[情形]，一年中遇到吉祥的[日子]，[人們]急於結婚，於是用紗巾蒙住姑娘的頭，夫家[把她]接過來。拜見公婆，就算[完成了]婚禮，[傳統婚禮當經歷的]六禮都捨去了。成婚的儀式倘被省棄，就用蒙首的辦法[來代替]，這也流傳很久了。只是古代有時是為臨時急於娶新娘而用的，可現在卻成了婚禮上通行的儀式了。

26   Bridal Veil[1]

At weddings nowadays, the bride's head is veiled under a red kerchief. As Du You explains in his Encyclopedia, "Beginning in the Eastern Han and Wei and Jin Dynasties, there were often hard times. Taking advantage of an auspicious day, people married hastily. A silk scarf was thrown over the bride's head and she was hastened to the groom's house. The proper *kowtowing* to the husband's parents completed, she was married there. The six etiquettes[2] that had hitherto been considered necessary had been abandoned." Without the six etiquettes, the practice of covering the bride's head has long since become the surrogate rite. The kerchief that was expedient for hasty weddings in ancient times is now a requirement in all weddings.

Zhao Yi (Qing Dynasty):
The Gaiyu Researches

【註釋】

1. 新娘蒙首：蒙首，也稱"蓋頭"。新婚時，要用紅色的手帕、紗巾、或鳳冠等將新娘的頭臉遮住。此古婚俗起源很早，流行於南北各地。

2. 六禮：古代在確立婚姻過程中的六種禮儀，即納采、問名、納吉、納徵、請期、親迎。

3. 合卺：原為古時婚禮的一種儀式，後用以指成婚。

Notes:

1. Bridal veil: also called the head cover. At the wedding, the bride's head and face should be covered by a red handkerchief, a scarf or a phoenix headdress. This custom originated a long time ago in many parts of China.

2. six etiquettes: In ancient times at a wedding, six etiquettes were necessary for the nuptials. They were: acceptance of the betrothal gifts, asking each other's name, picking an auspicious date, exchange of wedding gifts, sending out invitations and receiving the bride.

二十七　傳袋求子[1]

今人家娶婦，輿轎迎至大門，則傳席以入，弗令履地。然唐人已爾。

明　陶宗儀《南村輟耕錄》

今杭俗以米袋承氈，名曰"傳袋"，又曰"袋袋相傳"，以袋隱代。

清　金埴《不下帶篇》

【語譯】

現在人家裏娶媳婦，花轎[把新娘]迎到了大門口，就[用]氈席[鋪地，隨新娘的腳步次第]把氈席向前傳，直入家屋內，為了不[讓新娘的腳]着地。如此[習俗]唐代已有了。

當今杭州人的婚俗用米袋代替氈席，名叫"傳袋"，又叫作"袋袋相傳"，這是用"袋"字暗指"代"的意思。

27 Passing over Bags for an Offspring[1]

Nowadays at weddings when the bridal sedan chair reaches the gate, people spread felt mats in the gateway. They pass the mats on which the bride has walked successively to the front from behind for her to walk along. This custom started in the Tang Dynasty.

Tao Zongyi (Ming Dynasty):
Records of Stopping Farming in South Village

Now people in Hangzhou popularly use ricebags to replace felt mats. This custom is called "passing over the bags", or "passing over bags after bags". The word "bags" here serves as a pun for the word "generations".

Jin Zhi (Qing Dynasty):
The Buxiadai Writings

【註釋】

1. 傳袋求子：傳袋，也稱"傳代"、"傳席"。舊時流行於全國各地的婚禮儀式。婚娶人家必須用口袋鋪地，讓新娘踏在袋上進入婆家，新娘的腳不能沾地，否則不吉利。這種習俗是唐代以來的"傳席"習俗演變而來的。"袋"與"代"諧音，此儀式有傳宗接代吉兆的含義。

Notes:

1. Passing over bags for an offspring: "passing over bags", or "passing over mats", a marital rite practised in all parts of China in the old times. The groom's family would cover the doorway with felt rugs, straw mats or cloth bags. The bride stepped on these things as she entered the house. Her feet were not allowed to touch the bare ground, otherwise it was regarded as inauspicious. This custom developed from mat passing in the Tang Dynasty. "Bag" is a pun on "generation" in Chinese. This rite signifies the production of offsprings generation after generation.

二十八　拜堂[1]──　撒帳[2]──　合髻──喝交杯酒

　　二家各出彩緞，綰一同心[3]，謂之“牽巾”，男掛于笏[4]，女搭于手，男倒行出，面皆相向，至家廟[5]前參拜畢，女復倒行，扶入房中講拜，男女各爭先後對拜畢，就牀。女向左坐，男向右坐，婦女以金錢彩果散擲，謂之“撒帳”。男左女右，留少頭髮，二家出正段、釵子、木梳、頭須之類，謂之“合髻”。然後，用兩盞以彩結連之，互飲一盞，謂之“交杯酒”，飲訖擲盞，并花冠子于牀下，盞一仰一合，俗云：“大吉”，則眾喜賀。

宋　孟元老《東京夢華錄》

【語譯】

　　[男女] 兩家各出一段彩綢，[把它] 盤繞起來編成一個同心結，這叫“牽巾”。新郎 [把牽巾的一端] 掛在手板上，新娘 [把牽巾的另一端]搭在手上。新郎倒着 [牽新娘] 走，二人相向而行，到家廟前拜過祖先後，新娘再倒着走回房去。被人扶着，[新人] 行夫妻拜見禮，[通常] 二人 [都會] 爭先行禮。對拜結束，[他們] 就牀而坐，女人向左坐，男人向右坐。

　　婦女們用小錢幣，五色乾果 [向新婚夫婦] 撒去，這叫做“撒

28 *Bai Tang*[1], *Sa Zhang*[2], *He Ji* and Drinking *Jiao Bei* Wine

As the most important part of the wedding celebration, each family brings a length of silk and these are tied together to make a concentric knot[3]. This is called the "leading scarf". The bridegroom hangs one end of the scarf on his hand plate[4], while the bride holds the other end in her hand. The groom walks backwards, guiding the bride face to face, out of the room. After paying homage to the ancestors in the *jia miao*[5], the bride walks backwards to the nuptial chamber. With their arms supported by the maids, the bride and the groom try to be the first to salute each other. After this, they sit on the edge of the bed, the bride on the left, the groom on the right.

Women sprinkle coins and all kinds of dried fruit and nuts around them. This is called *sa zhang*.

People bind together a strand of the groom's hair on the left side of his head with that of the bride on the right side. Both families offer bolts of silk, hairpins, and other decorations for the head and put them together. This procedure is called *he ji*.

Afterwards, two tiny wine cups are tied together with a colourful silk string and the newlyweds drink the wine together. This practice is called "drinking *jiao bei* wine". Then

帳"。

把新郎左邊的 [一小股] 頭髮，新娘右邊的 [一小股] 頭髮合起來，雙方的家庭拿出一疋疋綢子、釵子、木梳和頭飾等物，這叫"合髻"。

此後，又用彩色的綢帶聯結住兩個小酒盅，新人互喝下一小杯酒，這稱為"交杯酒"，喝後，再把酒杯和花冠一起扔到牀下去，[如果發現]，一個杯口朝上，一個杯口朝下，便認為是"大吉利"[的徵兆]，於是，眾人 [紛紛向他們] 道喜祝賀。

【註釋】

1. 拜堂：新郎新娘在婚禮上的重要儀式，參拜天地父母祖先以及夫妻對拜。

2. 撒帳：民間婚禮習俗，向新婚夫婦撒五彩乾果或雜糧，表示喜慶祝願，原有驅邪避煞之意。

3. 同心：即同心結。傳統用絲綢帶編成的連環回文樣式的結子，以象徵堅貞的愛情。

4. 笏：手板。古代臣子朝見天子時手中拿的狹長板，可用來記事。後來的婚禮上即用類似的手板給新郎作為裝飾物。

5. 家廟：祭祀祖先的場所。

they throw the cups and the decorated head-dresses underneath the bed. If it happens that one cup faces upwards and the other downwards, it is regarded as auspicious and the wedding guests will congratulate them.

Meng Yuanlao (Song Dynasty):
Records of Dreams in East Capital

Notes:

1. *bai tang*: the most important ritual in the wedding, with the bride and the groom saluting Heaven and Earth, both parents, and each other.

2. *sa zhang*: a wedding folk custom. People throw colourful dried fruit and grains at the newlyweds to extend their good wishes and congratulations. It is also intended to drive away evil spirits.

3. concentric knot: a knot tied into concentric rings with silk threads. It symbolizes faithful love.

4. hand plate: or *hu*, a narrow plaque. Officials in the feudal times carried it to record things during an audience with the Emperor. It was used at weddings as a decoration for the bridegroom.

5. *jia miao*: or the family temple, a place where the family offers sacrifices to the ancestors.

二十九　鬧新房 [1]

新婦既入洞房，男女賓咸入，以欲搏新婦之笑，謔浪
笑敖，無所不至。……成年者之鬧房，其目的則在侮弄新
娘及伴房之女 [2]，淫詞戲語，信口而出，或評新娘頭足，或
以新娘脂粉塗飾他人之面，任意調笑，興盡而止。

徐珂《清稗類鈔》

【語譯】

新娘進了新房，男女客人都 [跟了] 進去，為了要搏得新娘的
笑容，[大家] 肆意 [和她] 開玩笑、嬉鬧，無所不為。……成年人
鬧新房的目的在於戲弄新娘和伴娘。[他們往往] 隨口說出 [一些]
庸俗下流的笑話；有的人對新娘評頭品足；有的人 [甚至] 把新娘
臉上的脂粉塗到了別人的臉上，任意地挑逗開玩笑，直到興盡才
停止。

【註釋】

1. 鬧新房：流行於南北各地的婚俗。除了表示祝賀外，人們常常將新郎
   和新娘作為開玩笑的對象。
2. 伴房之女：舊時舉行婚禮時陪伴照顧新娘的女子。

88

29　Teasing the Newlyweds

Soon after the newlyweds have entered the nuptial chamber, all the wedding guests, male and female, follow. To win the smiles of the bride, people wilfully tease her with all kinds of ridicule and jokes. This practice of foolery and frivolity by adults in the nuptial chamber is intended to embarrass the bride and the bridesmaid. The guests crack vulgar jokes in bawdy language and make flippant remarks about the bride's appearance. They go so far as to take the rouge and powder off the bride's face and put it on one another. They do not stop until they have had their fill of wanton fun and foolery.

Xu Ke: Classified Anecdotes of the Qing Dynasty

三十　回門[1]

其兩新人于三日或七朝九日，往女家行拜門禮。女親家設華筵，款待新婿。

宋　吳自牧《夢粱錄》

【語譯】

　　每對新婚夫婦在[婚後的]第三天或是第七天或是第九天，到新娘家去行拜門禮。新娘父母要舉行豐盛的宴會來款待新女婿。

【註釋】

1. 回門：新娘嫁到丈夫家俗稱"進門"，從夫家回到娘家故稱"回門"。此流行全國許多地區的婚姻習俗，含有兒女不忘父母養育之恩，女婿感謝岳父母，以及表示夫妻恩愛的意思。

30   Returning Home[1]

All newlyweds pay a formal visit to the bride's parents on the third, seventh or ninth day after the wedding. The bride's parents hold a bountiful feast to entertain the new son-in-law.

Wu Zimu (Song Dynasty):
Records of a Pipe Dream

Notes:

1. Returning home: When a bride is married, it is customarily called "entering (the bridegroom's) home"; therefore, when the newlyweds pay a formal visit to the bride's parents after the wedding, it is called "(the bride's) returning home". This custom is widely practised in all parts of China. It signifies the daughter's not forgetting her parental upbringing, the son-in-law's gratitude to his parents-in-law, and conjugal love between the newlyweds.

三十一　拋彩球[1]

　　交趾[2]俗，上巳日[3]男女聚會，各為行列，以五色結為球，歌而拋之，謂之"飛駝"。男女目成，則女受駝，而男婚已定。

　　　　　　　　　　宋　周去非《嶺南代答》

【語譯】

　　嶺南一帶的習俗，在夏曆三月初三那天，青年男女聚在一起，[按男女性別] 分別排成兩隊。用五彩綢布結成一個球，一邊唱歌，一邊把它拋出去，這稱作"飛駝"。男女青年 [雙方有意] 用眼睛 [傳情] 決定，女子接受了 [拋來的] 球，男方的婚事就算定下了。

【註釋】

1. 拋彩球：用拋彩球的方式來選擇配偶，原為南方少數民族的習俗，男拋女受。然而以後在中原地區的文學作品中大量出現的是女子拋繡球擇婿的故事。
2. 交趾：古代的地區名，泛指五嶺以南的地區。
3. 上巳日：夏曆三月初三。南方少數民族的傳統節日。

31 Tossing Colourful Balls[1]

In the Ling Nan area, on the third day of the third month in the lunar year, there is a gathering of young men and women. Forming two lines differentiated by sex, they play with a ball of knotted five-coloured silk cloth. While singing, they toss the ball. This gesture is called *fei tuo*. Messages are conveyed by eye contact between the young men and the young women. If a girl chooses to catch the ball, a marriage is probable.

Zhou Qufei (Song Dynasty):
Replies in Ling Nan

Notes:

1. Tossing colourful balls: a way of picking one's mate. Originally, it was a custom of the minority nationalities in the southern parts of China with men throwing and women catching the ball. Later, in the literary works of northern China there are many stories about women throwing the ball to select their future husbands.

三十二　鬧喪[1]

杭俗出殯前一夕，大家則唱戲宴客，謂之暖喪。吳中小民家，亦用鼓樂竟夜，親鄰畢集，謂之伴大夜。

清　慵訥居士《咫聞錄》

舊俗歿之夕，其家置酒食邀親友，鳴金伐鐃，歌呼達旦，或一夕或三五夕，謂之暖喪。

清（同治）《巴東縣志》

【語譯】

杭州的風俗在出殯前一天晚上，大戶人家就要 [請戲班子] 唱戲，宴請賓客。這稱之為"暖喪"。吳地一帶的小戶人家，[出殯前夕] 也整夜地演奏鼓樂，親戚鄰人都聚集在一起，這稱作"伴大夜"。

舊時的習俗，人去世的這夜，他的家人要準備酒和食物邀請親戚朋友來家裏，他們敲打金屬的樂器，唱啊叫啊直到天亮，有的家用一夜，有的家用三夜 [甚至用] 五夜。這稱作"暖喪"。

32 Clamorous Funeral[1]

On the eve of the funeral procession, it is a local custom in Hangzhou that rich families invite a theatrical troupe to put on a performance and entertain their guests at feasts in their houses. This practice is called a "warm funeral". Lesser families in the Wu area also have people play music accompanied by drumbeats. All their relatives and neighbours gather. This practice is called "accompanying through the major night".

Lay Buddhist Yong Na (Qing Dynasty):
A Record of Hearsay in the Vicinity

It is an old custom that on the night of someone's death, a wake is arranged in his house to entertain relatives and friends. People beat drums and gongs and sing songs till daybreak. Some families do so for one night, whereas others go on for three to five nights. This practice is called a "warm funeral".

(Qing Dynasty in the Year of Tongzhi):
County Annals of Badong

【註釋】

1. 鬧喪：也稱為"暖喪"、"坐夜"、"伴大夜"。流行於南方的喪葬習俗。這本是古代輓歌的遺迹，後來已經漸漸失去了原來的樣子。

Notes:

1. Clamorous funeral: also referred to as a "warm funeral", "sitting up through the night", or "accompanying through the major night". This is a funeral custom observed in the southern parts of China. The chants and music are vestiges of the dirges of ancient times.

三十三　做七[1]

　　或問：人死，每遇七日則作佛事，謂之做七，何歟？
曰：人生四十九日而魄生，亦四十九日而魄散。……曰：
然則做佛事亦有益歟？曰：此俗尚也，愚夫愚婦之所為
也。

清　王應奎《柳南隨筆》

【語譯】

　　有人問：人死了，每逢七天就要作佛事，稱之為做七，為甚
麼呢？回答說：人出生後四十九天魂魄才生成，魂魄散去也要四
十九天。問：然而做佛事也是有好處的吧？回答說：這只是習俗
罷了，無知無識的男女所做的事。

【註釋】

1. 做七：人死後每隔七天，作一次佛事，紀念死者，依次到七七四十九
   天而止。此喪葬習俗至今流行全國。

33   Doing the Sevenths[1]

One may ask, "When people die, religious ceremonies are held every seventh day. This custom is called 'doing the sevenths'. Why is it necessary?" The answer is, "The soul of a human is formed in the forty-nine days after his birth and it also takes forty-nine days for one's soul to disperse". Question: But is there any benefit in holding these ceremonies at all? Answer: This is only a local custom. It is observed by the illiterate.

Wang Yingkui (Qing Dynasty):
Jottings in Liu Nan

Notes:

1. Doing the sevenths: After one's death, a religious ceremony is held by his family members and relatives every seventh day for seven times to commemorate the dead. The ceremonies last for forty-nine days in all. This funeral custom is observed all over China even today.

三十四 鬼婚[1]

　　山西石州風俗，凡男子未娶而死，其父母俟公大有女死，必求之以配之，議婚定禮[2]納幣，率如生者，葬日亦復宴會親戚，女死，父母欲為贅婿，禮亦如之。

明　陸容《菽園雜記》

【語譯】

　　山西石州的風俗，凡是男子還未娶親就死了，他的父母等到社會地位高的人家有女兒去世，一定前去求婚請求配成[夫妻]。議婚、送定禮、下聘禮，全和活着的人一樣。[結成鬼婚的兩個死者]下葬的那天要再次宴請親戚。女子死了，她的父母想為她招女婿，[入贅]禮儀也和[活着的人]一樣。

【註釋】

1. 鬼婚：俗稱"攀陰親"、"冥婚"。民間認為，人死後在冥界生活與現世人間是一樣的，故為去世的未婚男女擇偶相配。
2. 定禮：指訂婚的禮金。

34　Ghost Marriage[1]

It is a local custom in Shizhou, Shanxi Province, that if a man dies before getting married, his parents will wait to make a marriage proposal for him when the daughter of a powerful family dies. Then they will negotiate the wedding, and then offer bethothal gifts and money, just as they do for the living. On the day of burial of the two, banquets are held to entertain the relatives. Likewise, if a young woman dies, her parents will look for a deceased husband for her. The *ru zhui*[2] rites are the same as those for the living.

Lu Rong (Ming Dynasty):
Assorted Notes in a Pepper Garden

Notes:

1. Ghost marriage: customarily called "arranging a nether marriage" or simply "nether world marriage". Folk people believe that life in the nether world is the same as in this world. Therefore, they arrange marriages for deceased single men and women.

2. *ru zhui*: Rarely in China the son-in-law marries a girl and lives in her parents' house. This kind of matrilocal marriage takes the special term "*ru zhui*".

三十五　做冥壽[1]

祝壽者，祝其人之長生不死也。乃有為已卒之祖父母、父母稱觴祝壽者，曰冥壽，也曰冥慶。

徐珂《清稗類鈔》

南州宗室謂親死日為暗忌，生日為明忌，宗中極重明忌。親死者遇日生日，如五十、六十之類，猶追壽焉。族人具禮謁賀，一如存日。

清　翟灝《通俗編》

【語譯】

祝壽，是祝人長生不死。還有為已經去世的祖父母和父母舉杯祝壽的，稱為做冥壽，也稱作冥慶。

南州皇族稱親人去世的日子為"暗忌"，生日叫"明忌"，族中人非常重視明忌。遇到親人中死者的生日，例如五十、六十之類，像是追加壽命似的，族中的人準備禮物拜謁祝賀，如同他活着一樣。

【註釋】

1. 做冥壽：給死人做生日、祝壽。在已故的長輩誕辰時，舉行祝壽禮儀，儀式如同做陽壽。舊時流行於全國大部份地區的習俗。

35 Celebrating the Nether Birthday[1]

To celebrate someone's birthday is to wish him longevity. But people also drink to their deceased parents and grandparents as a birthday wish. This practice is called "celebrating the nether birthday".

Xu Ke (Qing Dynasty):
Classified Anecdotes of the Qing Dynasty

Among the imperial clans of Nanzhou, the anniversary of the death of a person is called the "dark anniversary", whereas the anniversary of his birth is called the "bright anniversary". Clansmen attach much importance to the bright anniversary. When important birthdays (like the fiftieth or sixtieth) of the deceased take place, they are regarded as an extension of life. Clansmen still present gifts and congratulations as if the person were alive.

Zhai Hao (Qing Dynasty):
Articles on Popular Things

Notes:

1. Celebrating the nether birthday: The rites for celebrating the birthday of deceased elders of the family are the same as those for the living. This was a custom practised in most parts of China in the old times.

三十六　摸秋求子[1]

　　女伴秋夜出游，各于瓜田摘瓜歸，為宜男兆，名曰摸秋。

清　梁紹壬《兩般秋雨庵隨筆》

　　金陵俗，中秋月夜婦女有"摸秋"之戲。嘗往茉莉園，以得瓜豆宜男。

潘宗鼎《金陵歲時記》

【語譯】

　　婦女結伴在秋夜出門遊玩，各人在瓜田 [摸着] 摘一個瓜回家，[據說這] 是生男孩的徵兆。[這種風俗] 名叫"摸秋"。

　　南京的風俗，中秋節的月夜婦女有摸秋的遊戲，她們去茉莉園試着 [暗中摸索]，摸到了瓜豆，[就被認為] 是生男孩的 [吉兆]。

【註釋】

1. 摸秋求子：夏曆八月十五夜，婦女到田野的瓜架、豆棚下暗中摸索瓜豆，傳說摸到南瓜易生男孩，因為"南瓜"和"男娃"諧音，摸到扁豆則易生女孩。習俗規定這天瓜豆的主人不得責怪摸秋的婦女。

104

36   Touching the Autumn for a Son[1]

Women go out in groups on an autumn night. Each picks a melon by groping in the field and takes it home. People regard success in this endeavour as a lucky sign of having a boy. This practice is called "touching the autumn".

Liang Shaoren (Qing Dynasty):
Jottings in "Autumn Rain Hut of a Different Kind"

It is a folk custom of Nanjing that women play a game called "touching the autumn" on Mid-Autumn night. They grope in the dark in the fields of Jasmine Garden. If they get melons or beans, it is regarded as an auspicious sign foretelling the bearing of a boy.

Pan Zongding: An Annual Record of Jinling

Notes:

1. Touching the autumn for a son: On the night of August 15th of the lunar year, women grope in the dark under the trellises of melons and beans. It is believed that if a woman gets a pumpkin, she is likely to bear a boy. This is because the word "pumpkin" in Chinese is homonymous with the word "boy". If one gets a bean, she is likely to have a girl. The folk custom also stipulates that the owner of the melons and beans should not blame women for "touching the autumn".

三十七　催生禮[1]

　　杭城人家育子，如孕婦入月，期將屆，外舅姑家以銀盆或彩盆，盛粟杆一束，上以錦或紙蓋之，上簇花朵、通草、貼套，五男二女意思，及眠羊臥鹿[2]，并以彩畫鴨蛋一百二十枚、膳食、羊、生棗、栗果，及孩兒繡繃彩衣，送至婿家，名“催生禮”。

宋　吳自牧《夢粱錄》

【語譯】

　　杭州城裏人家生孩子，如孕婦[懷孕]進入最後一個月，產期將到的時候，娘家人就用銀盆或彩色的盆盛一束粟米桿子，上面蓋着絲綢或紙，並用花朵、通草交織的花樣點綴着，表示生育五男二女的意思。還有麵粉做的睡羊和臥鹿、一百二十個彩繪的鴨蛋、日常的飯菜、羊、未熟的棗子、栗子和手繡的彩色嬰兒服裝送到女婿家中，這叫作“催生禮”。

【註釋】

1. 催生禮：娘家送給臨產的女兒的禮物。流行於江南等地的生育習俗。
2. 眠羊臥鹿：宋代一種麵製的食品，做成睡着的羊、臥着的鹿的樣子。

37 Gifts Expediting Child Delivery[1]

As families in Hangzhou await a child in a woman's last month of pregnancy, just before delivery members of the family will place a bunch of millet stalks in a silver or an ornamental pot covered with silk or paper and decorated with interwoven patterns of flowers and rice-paper plant. This suggests chances of bearing five boys and two girls. In addition, there are pastries in the shape of sleeping lambs and crouching deer, one hundred and twenty painted duck eggs, regular dishes, lamb, raw dates and chestnuts and embroidered clothes for the infant. All these are sent to the son-in-law's house. They are called "gifts expediting child delivery".

Wu Zimu (Song Dynasty):
Records of a Pipe Dream

Notes:

1. Gifts expediting child delivery: These are gifts from the woman's family before her delivery. This is a birth custom practised in parts of China south of the Yangtze River.

三十八 滿月洗兒會[1]

　　親朋俱集，煎香湯于銀盆內，下洗兒果彩錢等，仍用
色彩繞盆，謂之"圍盆紅"。尊長以金銀釵攪水，名曰
"攪盆釵"。親賓亦以金錢銀釵撒于盆內，謂之"添
盆"。盆內有立棗兒，少年婦爭取而食之，以為生男之
徵。浴兒落胎髮畢，以髮入金銀小盒，……抱兒遍謝諸親
坐客。……若富室宦家，則用此禮。貧下之家，則隨其
儉。

宋　吳自牧《夢粱錄》

【語譯】

　　[孩子滿月那天]，親戚朋友全都聚集在一起，[家人] 把和着香
料煮好的熱水 [倒] 在銀盆裏，把 [叫作]"洗兒果"[的乾果] 和彩
色的錢幣等放在水裏，還用彩色的絲綢繞在盆上，這稱作"圍盆
紅"。長輩用金釵或銀釵攪 [盆中的] 水，這名叫"攪盆釵"。客人
中的近親也把金的錢幣、銀的釵撒到盆中去，這叫作"添盆"。盆
水中 [若浮] 有豎立着的棗子，年輕的婦人都爭着拿來吃掉，[她
們] 認為這是生男孩的徵兆。洗完孩子，剃完胎髮，把胎髮放入金
或銀製成的小盒中。[大人] 抱着孩子感謝每個親人和客人。倘是
有錢的人家或者是官宦人家，就用這樣的禮儀，普通的人或窮困
的人家，隨自己 [的能力] 節儉一些。

38 Child Bathing at One Month Old[1]

When an infant is one month old, relatives and friends gather in the house. These people pour warm scented water into a silver pot, and put nuts called "infant-bathing nuts" and colourful paper notes in the water. They tie bright silks around the pot. These silks are called "red around the pot". Elder members stir the water in the pot with gold or silver hairpins. These are called "pot stirring pins". The close relatives among the guests drop gold coins or silver pins into the pot. This practice is called "adding to the pot". If there are dates floating upright in the water, young women race to eat them, because they think doing so foretells their having a boy. After bathing the infant, people shave its head and collect its hair in a gold or silver box. Parents then show the baby around to thank all those attending. This rite is adopted by rich families and families of officials. Common people and poor families have something simpler in accordance with their economic means.

Wu Zimu (Song Dynasty):
Records of a Pipe Dream

【註釋】

1. 洗兒會：通常在嬰兒滿月時舉行，家庭對新生嬰兒祝福的重要儀式。
   舊時漢族的生育習俗。現時，家長對嬰孩滿月一般也很重視，亦有人
   家擺"滿月酒"，以示慶祝。

Notes:

1. Child bathing at one month old: When a baby was one month old, a child-bathing ceremony was performed as a blessing for the baby. Nowadays parents still consider the first moon of a baby's birth important. Though some old rites are dropped, many families still hold "Full Moon Banquets" as a celebration.

三十九　抓周試兒 [1]

　　至來歲生日，謂之“周晬”，羅列盤盞于地，盛果木、飲食、官誥、筆研、算秤等經卷針綫應用之物，觀其所先拈者，以為徵兆，謂之“試晬”。此小兒之盛禮也。

宋　孟元老《東京夢華錄》

【語譯】

　　到 [小孩] 第二年生日，稱作“滿週歲”。[家裏人把] 盤子、淺碗一個個排在地上，裏面盛着果子、吃的東西、官府的文告、筆硯、籌子、秤、以及書籍、針綫等等 [各種各樣的] 用的東西，觀察孩子所先抓取的是甚麼，把這作為 [他將來志趣的] 徵兆，這叫作“週歲試兒”。這是小孩的一個盛大儀式。

【註釋】

1. 抓周試兒：一種預測小兒性情、志趣和前途的民間儀式，此習俗早在北齊就已形成，流行全國各地。

39   A Vocational Inclination Test for an Infant[1]

On its second birthday, a child is said to have "reached a full year". Members of the family array dishes and bowls on the ground. They contain various useful items such as fruit and nuts, edibles, official documents, pens and inkstands, tokens and scales, books and scrolls, needles and threads. People then observe closely what the baby grabs first. They take it as a sign of his future vocational inclination. This practice is called "lot-drawing to test a child". This is a grand occasion for the child.

Meng Yuanlao (Song Dynasty):
Records of Dreams in East Capital

Notes:

1. A vocational inclination test for an infant: This is a folk ceremony to predict a child's temperament, inclination and prospects. This custom grew up in the Northern Qi time (6th century) and is popularly observed all over China.

四十　寄名神鬼 [1]

　　懼兒夭殤，……且有寄名于神鬼如觀音大士、文昌帝君、城隍土地、且及于無常 [2] 是也，或即寄名于僧尼，而亦皆稱之于乾親家 [3]。

徐珂《清稗類鈔》

【語譯】

　　擔心幼兒夭折，[家長] 就 [將孩子] 在神鬼前"寄名"作弟子，如觀音菩薩、文昌帝君、城隍、土地等，甚至無常鬼也可以。有的就拜和尚、尼姑為師，而且也稱他們為"乾親家"。

【註釋】

1. 寄名：為了求得孩子長命而讓孩子拜神鬼或僧道為師，但不出家。舊時育兒的一種風俗，流行全國各地。
2. 無常：傳說中的勾魂鬼。
3. 乾親家：沒有血緣關係而結成的親戚。

40 Dedicating to Deities and Spirits[1]

For fear of premature death of their child, parents dedicate him or her as a disciple to deities and spirits like the Guanyin Buddha, the Wenchang Emperor, the god of the town and the earth god[2], or sometimes even to Impermanence[3]. Other people just acknowledge monks or nuns as masters and address them as honorary relatives.

Xu Ke: Classified Anecdotes of the Qing Dynasty

Notes:

1. Dedicating to deities and spirits: To wish longevity for the child, parents make their children acknowledge deities and spirits or monks and nuns as masters, but the children do not become monks or nuns. This was a child-raising custom prastised widely in China in the old times.

2. Guanyin Buddha, ...earth god: These deities and spirits are commonly believed to be people's guardians and protectors.

3. Impermanence: a lengendary ghost which snatches souls.

四十一　指腹婚[1]

　　世俗，好于襁褓[2]童幼之時輕許為婚，亦有指腹為婚者。及其既長，或不肖無賴，或身有惡疾，或家貧凍餒或喪服相仍，或從宦遠方，遂至背信棄約，速獄致訟者多矣。

　　　　　　　　　　宋　司馬光《司馬氏書議》

【語譯】

　　按照民間風俗，[人們常] 喜歡輕率地為在襁褓中或尚在童年時代 [的子女] 定下婚姻，也有子女尚在母胎中就 [由父母] 訂婚的。等到孩子長大，有的人成了沒出息的無賴，有的人身患重病，有的家庭貧困挨凍受餓或者喪事不斷，有的 [離家] 去遠方做官，於是就產生了背棄以往的婚約 [的事件]，[因此] 而招致打官司爭辯是非曲直的人是很多的啊。

【註釋】

1. 指腹婚：指着懷着胎兒的腹部，雙方父母達成了子女的婚約。此習俗自漢代開始，流行時間甚長，現已杜絕。
2. 襁褓：包裹嬰兒的布或被。

41 "Belly-Pointing" Marriage[1]

An ill-advised folkway leads parents to arrange marriages for children still in diapers — or even in the womb. But babies can grow into problems: they may be good-for-nothing, or contract serious diseases; they may suffer the effects of cold or starvation brought on by poverty, or their families may be impoverished by many funerals; some may leave home for government posts in far-away places. Therefore in the fullness of time the engagements may be broken off, resulting in many breach-of-promise lawsuits.

Sima Guang (Song Dynasty):
Sima's Comments on Books

Notes:

1. "Belly-pointing" marriage: a marriage agreement made by parents for the children still in the womb by pointing at the pregnant abdomens. The custom started in the Han Dynasty, but has been abandoned by now.

四十二　過房[1]

　　但習見閭閻里俗，養過房子及異姓乞養義男之類，畏
人知者，皆諱其所生父母。

　　　　　　　　　　　　　宋　歐陽修《歐陽文忠集》

【語譯】

　　常見到民間習俗，[有] 撫養兄弟或親戚的兒子以及不同姓的
人要求拜認為兒子的這類事，擔心別人知道的，都隱瞞孩子親生
父母 [的姓名]。

【註釋】

1. 過房：也稱"過繼"。因自己無子而撫養兄弟親戚的孩子，稱為"過
　房"。此本是中國宗族制度下的一種繼承制度，流行於全國。但習俗
　中至今仍常有為情感、利益等種種原因將沒有血緣關係的幼童收作
　"過房兒子"、"過房女兒"的(也稱"乾兒子"、"乾女兒")。

42   Transfer of House[1]

Often seen is a folk custom that a person adopts a son from his brother or a relative or from someone of a different family name. Those who are afraid of their practice being known to others conceal the names of the natural parents.

Ouyang Xiu (Song Dynasty):
Collected Works of Ouyang Wenzhong

Notes:

1. Transfer of house: If someone does not have a son, he usually adopts one from his brother or his relatives or from other people of a different family name. This practice is called "transfer of house" This was a system of family succession practised in the clansman times in China. But it is also customary to adopt children of no blood relation. These adoptees are known as "transferred" sons or daughters — taken in for charitable or economic motives.

四十三　十二生肖 [1]

　　蓋北俗初無所謂子丑寅卯之十二辰 [2]，但以鼠牛虎兔之類分紀歲時，浸尋流傳中國 [3]，遂相沿不廢耳。

清　趙翼《陔餘叢考》

【語譯】

　　北方 [少數民族] 的習俗最初並沒有子丑寅卯等 [用以計時的] 十二辰，只是用鼠牛虎兔之類 [動物來] 區分記錄年月，[這] 漸漸地傳到中原地區並和 [中原記時法] 結合，於是 [十二生肖] 就代代相傳沒有再廢棄。

【註釋】

1. 十二生肖：古代以農業生產不可缺少的曆算十二地支，配以一個相應的動物，組成了子鼠、丑牛、寅虎、卯兔、辰龍、巳蛇、午馬、未羊、申猴、酉雞、戌狗、亥豬十二屬相，後來習俗即以人出生在那年即為屬某動物。

2. 十二辰：即子、丑、寅、卯、辰、巳、午、未、申、酉、戌、亥十二地支，古代用以記年月日時等時間，為中原記時法。

3. 中國：上古時代，我國華夏族建國於黃河流域一帶，以為居天下之中，故稱中國，而把周圍地區稱作四方。後即用中國泛指中原地區。

43 Twelve Animals Representing Twelve Earthly Branches[1]

The minority nationalities in the northern part of China originally did not adopt the twelve zodiacal Earthly Branches[2]. Instead, they used animals like the rat, the ox, the tiger and the rabbit to designate years. Later, the animal sign system gradually combined with the Earthly Branches system that was practised in the Central Plains[3] and is passed down through the generations to the present day.

Zhao Yi (Qing Dynasty):
The Gaiyu Researches

Notes:

1. Twelve animals representing twelve Earthly Branches: These are the twelve Earthly Branches used in farming almanacs in ancient times, paired with the twelve animal symbols. They are: Zi-Rat; Chou-Ox; Yin-Tiger; Mao-Rabbit; Cheng-Dragon; Si-Snake; Wu-Horse; Wei-Sheep; Shen-Monkey; You-Cock; Xu-Dog and Hai-Boar. Currently, one still identifies the year in which one was born by referring to one of the twelve animals.

2. the twelve zodiacal Earthly Branches: They are used in combination with the ten Heavenly Stems to designate years, months, days and hours.

3. Central Plains: referring to northern China.

四十四　觀音生日[1]

　　十九日，為觀音誕辰。士女駢集殿庭炷香，或施佛前長明燈油，以保安康。或供長幡，云求子得子。既生小兒，則于觀音座下皈依寄名[2]，可保長壽。僧尼建觀音會，莊嚴道場[3]，香花供養。婦女自二月朔[4]持齋[5]，至是日止，俗呼觀音素。六月九月朔至十九日，皆如之。

清　顧祿《清嘉錄》

【語譯】

　　[夏曆二月]十九日是觀音菩薩的生日。成雙結對的男女聚集在[佛寺的]大殿或庭院中焚香[禮拜]。有的人送上佛像前長明燈的油，為了[祈求觀音]保佑[他們]平安健康；有的人供上長幡，據說[因此]可求子得子。生孩子[的人]，就到觀音的[蓮]座下表示依附歸順，[讓孩子]作觀音的義子，[傳說這樣]可保佑人長壽。和尚尼姑所設立的觀音會，道場[氣氛]莊嚴，[並有]香和花來奉祀。

　　婦女們從二月初一起吃齋到這天結束，俗稱為"觀音素"。[不僅如此]、[每逢夏曆]六月、九月的初一到十九，也都這樣吃齋。

44   The Birthday of Guanyin[1]

The nineteenth day of the second month of the lunar year is the birthday of Guanyin. On that day, young men and women gather to burn joss sticks and worship either in the temple hall or in the court area. Some offer oil for Guanyin's ever-burning lamp and pray for health and peace; others offer long silk scrolls in the hope of bearing a son. If a son is born, the parents will put him under Guanyin's lotus seat to proclaim their faith in Buddhism and make the baby the adopted child of Guanyin[2]. By doing so, they think Guanyin will bless the child with longevity. Monks and nuns set up assemblies in honour of Guanyin. The places of worship are solemn and grand. Incense and flowers are also offered to Guanyin.

Women eat a vegetarian diet from the first until the nineteenth of the second month, the birthday of Guanyin. This is called Guanyin's vegetarian fast. This practice is observed again from 1st to 19th of the sixth and the ninth months in the lunar year.

Gu Lu (Qing Dynasty):
Worthy Records of Qing Dynasty

123

【註釋】

1. 觀音生日：觀音，中國佛教四大菩薩之一。民間稱她為大慈大悲的菩薩，傳說如有難，只要誦其名，觀音即前往拯救解脱。夏曆二月十九日是觀音的生日，六月十九日是其成道日，九月十九日是其出家日，民間都有影響。

2. 寄名：為求孩子長命而認他人為義父母。參見第四十篇"寄名神鬼"。

3. 道場：佛教誦經禮拜的場所。

4. 朔：夏曆每月初一。

5. 持齋：即吃齋，吃素食。

Notes:

1. The Birthday of Guanyin: Guanyin is one of the four Buddhas in China. People believe her to be an infinitely merciful Buddha. It is said that in times of difficulty, if you chant her name, she will come to your rescue. February 19 of the lunar year is her birthday; June 19 is the anniversary of her enlightenment. On September 19, she ends her secular life and is transfigured into a Buddha. People hold ceremonies on these special days.

2. the adopted child of Guanyin: to seek longevity for their children, parents often dedicate them in symbolic adoption to divinities.

四十五　舍緣豆 [1]

四月八日，都人之好善者，取青黃豆數升，宣佛號 [2]
拈之。拈畢煮熟，散之市人，謂之舍緣豆。預結來世緣
也。

清　富察敦崇　《燕京歲時記》

先是拈豆唸佛，一豆，佛號一聲，有唸豆至石者。至
日熟豆，人遍舍之，其人亦一唸佛，啖一豆也。凡婦不見
答于夫姑婉若者，婢妾擯于主及姥者，則自咎曰：身前世
不舍豆兒，不結得人緣也。

明　劉侗　于奕正《帝京景物略》

【語譯】

夏曆四月初八，城裏喜歡行善的人，拿出幾升青豆或黃豆，
[一邊] 唸佛號 [一邊] 用手指拈一顆顆的豆。拈完以後把豆煮熟
了，分送給路上的人，這稱作"舍緣豆"，預示着結下一世的緣
份。

[佛誕日] 先是拈着豆唸佛，拈一顆豆唸一聲佛號。[甚至] 有
唸到一石豆 [這樣多的人]。到那天煮熟了豆，遍送給人，[得了豆

126

45 Distributing Predestination Beans[1]

On the eighth day the fourth lunar month, philanthropic people in cities go into the streets with several litres of green beans and yellow beans. They pinch each bean in turn and chant Buddha's name. Afterwards they boil the beans and offer them to the passers-by. These beans are called "predestination beans". They are believed to be able to pre-arrange favourable relationships in the next incarnation.

Fucha Duncong (Qing Dynasty):
Annual Records of the Capital

Prior to this date, people pinch the beans and chant Buddha's name: one bean, one chant. Some are able to process a hundred litres of beans. On the eighth day of the fourth month, they cook the beans and distribute them to the other people who also chant Buddha's name each time after eating a bean. Women who are snubbed by their mothers-in-law, or maids and concubines who fall out of favour with their masters or mistresses, will reprimand themselves by saying, "I am not welcome because I did not distribute beans in my former life".

Liu Tong and Yu Yizheng (Ming Dynasty):
Scenery and Events in the Capital

的] 那人也要唸一聲佛號，吃下一顆豆。凡是 [有] 得不到婆婆應答 [佛號] 的婦女，[或者作為] 婢女小妾 [捨緣豆但仍] 被主人或家中的女性長輩厭棄的人，就要自責說：“我前世沒捨豆兒，[所以今世] 結不到人緣啊。”

【註釋】

1. 捨緣豆：夏曆四月初八佛誕日的風俗活動之一。
2. 宣佛號：唸頌佛經中的頌詞。

Notes:

1. Distributing predestination beans: a customary activity held on April 8th of the lunar year, the birthday of Buddha.

四十六　香湯浴佛

四月八日為佛誕日，諸寺院各有浴佛會，僧尼輩競以小盆貯銅像，浸以糖水覆以花棚，鐃鈸[1]交迎，編往邸第富室，以小杓澆灌，以求施利。是日西湖作放生[2]會，舟楫甚盛，略如春時小舟[3]，競置龜魚螺蚌放生。

宋　周密《武林舊事》

【語譯】

四月八日是佛的生日，各個寺院中都有浴佛會，和尚尼姑這些人競相用小盆盛着銅佛像，把它浸在糖水裏，[上面]架起花棚，敲擊着鐃鈸，排着隊送[佛]去有錢人的府邸。[他們]用小杓澆洗佛像，為的是求得[富人]施捨錢物。這天西湖有放生會，船隻非常多，穿梭往來猶如春天[遊湖的]小船，[人們]爭着買龜、魚、螺、蚌來放生。

【註釋】

1. 鐃鈸：一種敲擊樂器。
2. 放生：釋放龜鳥等動物，信佛者的一種善舉。
3. 春時小舟：春天西湖上遊湖的小船頗多。這裏指人們到小船上去買水生動物用以放生的盛況。

46　Bathing Buddha in Aromatic Water

The eighth day of the fourth lunar month is the birthday of Buddha. Bathing Buddha ceremonies are held in every temple. Monks and nuns dip a copper statue of Buddha in a small basin of sweetened water. On top of the basin is a flower trellis. Forming lines to the clash of cymbals, the celebrants march to the homes of the rich to beg alms. On the same day, there is a ritualistic freeing of captive crustaceans and fish[1]. There are so many boats that they are like small pleasure crafts in spring shuttling back and forth. To gain merit, people vie in buying turtles, fish, snails and clams to set them free.

Zhou Mi (Song Dynasty):
Past Events of the Martial Arts World

Notes:

1. freeing captive crustaceans and fish: a philanthropic act of the Buddhists.

四十七　求雨

　　凡歲時不雨，家貼龍王神馬[1]于門，磁瓶插柳枝，掛門之傍，小兒塑泥龍，張紙旗擊鼓金，焚香各龍王廟。羣歌曰：“青龍頭，白龍頭，小兒求雨天歡喜。麥子麥子焦黃，起動起動龍王，大下小下，初一到十八……。”

明　劉侗　于奕正《帝京景物略》

【語譯】

　　凡是到一定的節令而沒下雨，家中的人就在門上貼上龍王的神像，把柳枝插在瓷瓶中掛在門旁邊。小孩用泥塑成龍的形狀，〔人們〕揮動紙旗，敲鑼打鼓，在各龍王廟燒香，一起唱歌：“青龍頭，白龍頭，小兒求雨天歡喜。麥子麥子焦黃，起動起動龍王，大下小下，初一到十八”。

【註釋】

1. 神馬：指神像。

47　Begging for Rain

During droughts, people put portraits of the Dragon King[1]
on their doors and insert willows branches in porcelain vases
which they hang by their doors. Children mould statues of
the Dragon King in clay. People wave paper flags, beat drums
and gongs and burn joss sticks in the Temple of the Dragon
King. Together they sing, "Green dragon head; white dragon
tail. Kids beg for rain and Heaven is pleased. The wheat is
scorched. This wakes the Dragon King. Small rains and big
rains pour from the start to the middle of the month".

Liu Tong and Yu Yizheng (Ming Dynasty):
Scenery and Events in the Capital

Notes:

1.　the Dragon King: the god of rain in Chinese mythology.

四十八　關公[1]誕

　　十三日為關帝生日，官為致祭于周太保橋之廟……十三日前，已割牲演劇，華鐙萬盞，拜禱為謹。……又相傳九月十三日為成神之辰，其儀一如五月十三日制。俗以此二日雨為關王磨刀雨，主人口平安。

清　顧祿《清嘉錄》

【語譯】

　　[夏曆五月] 十三日為關帝生日，官府在周太保橋 [那兒] 的廟祭祀關帝。十三日以前 [民間] 已經開始 [為祭祀而] 屠宰牲口演戲，萬盞彩燈光華燦爛，[人們] 謹慎小心地祭拜祈禱。還相傳九月十三日是關公成為神的日子，那天的儀式和五月十三日完全相同。民間認為這兩天裏下的雨是關公磨戰刀的雨水，預兆人們生活平安。

【註釋】

1. 關公：也稱"關帝"、"關王"、"關老爺"，是三國時代著名將領關羽（字雲長）神化的尊稱。關公受到人們普遍的崇拜，舊時各地都建有關帝廟、關廟。

48   The Birthday of Guan Gong[1]

The thirteenth day of the fifth lunar month is the birthday of Guan Gong. Local authorities offer sacrifices to him in the temple by the Zhou Tai Bao Bridge. People start buying meat and putting on performances before the 13th. Tens of thousands of bright lamps are lit. People worship with sincere prayers. It is also said that the thirteenth day of the ninth lunar month is the day when Guan Gong was apotheosized. The ceremonies on these two days are identical. It is popularly believed that if it rains on these days, it happens because Guan Gong is wetting the whetstone on which he sharpens his long-hilt sabre. The rain presages the well-being of the people.

Gu Lu (Qing Dynasty) :
Worthy Records of the Qing Dynasty

Notes:

1. Guan Gong (Master Guan): also referred to as Emperor Guan, King Guan, and the revered General Guan — respectful forms of address for a famous general of the Three Kingdoms Period (3rd century) in Chinese history. His proper name was Guan Yu, alias Guan Yunchang. Guan Gong is still popularly well-respected. Temples of Emperor Guan are set up in various places.

四十九 香市盛況 [1]

西湖香市，起于花朝 [2]，盡于端午 [3]。……香客 [4] 雜來，光景又別……如逃如逐，如奔如追，撩撥不開，牽挽不住，數百十萬男男女女，老老少少，日簇擁于寺之前後左右者，凡四閱月方罷。

清　張岱《陶庵夢憶》

【語譯】

西湖的香市從花朝節開始，端午節結束。[西湖的] 風景因香客紛紛而來，有另一種景象。幾百萬男男女女，老老少少像 [有人在] 追趕而奔跑，[想往前擠]，撥不開 [人羣]，[想] 拉住 [他們，也] 辦不到。[香客] 每天簇擁在佛寺的左右前後，這樣大致要經過四個月才停止。

【註釋】

1. 香市：拜佛者參加寺廟舉行的香會（進香活動），因其盛大，故稱香市。流行於浙江、江蘇、山東等地的民間信仰習俗。其中以杭州的西湖香市歷史最悠久、規模最繁盛。

2. 花朝：指夏曆二月十二日花朝節。相傳這一天是百花的生日。

3. 端午：即夏曆五月初五端午節。

4. 香客：民間對拜佛者的稱呼。香客在進香期間必須吃齋，多數香客都參加各地寺廟舉行的香會活動。

49 The Grand Occasion of Offering Joss Sticks[1]

In areas near the West Lake, the custom of offering joss sticks begins on the day of the Flower Festival[2] and ends on Dragon Boat Festival[3] Day. The scenery of the West Lake changes greatly with the arrival of pilgrims [4]. Millions of people, men and women, young and old, elbow and shove, jostling in vain through the crowd, snatching and slipping. Daily, the pilgrims throng the temples. This excitement lasts about four months.

Zhang Dai (Qing Dynasty) :
Memories of Dreams in Tao Recluse

Notes:

1. offering joss sticks: an occasion on which Buddhist pilgrims gather and go to burn joss sticks in temples. This is a religious custom popular in the Zhejiang, Jiangsu and Shandong provinces. The most long-standing and flourishing celebration is the one in the West Lake area of Hangzhou, Zhejiang Province.

2. Flower Festival: It comes on February 12 of the lunar year, said to be the birthday of all flowers.

3. Dragon Boat Festival: see Passage 14.

4. pilgrims: i.e., Buddhists. They practise abstinence from meat during the period of offering joss sticks. Most of the pilgrims also take part in the activities organized by the temples.

五十　送寒衣[1]

十月朔，……士民[2]家祭祖掃墓，如中元儀。晚夕緘
書冥楮，加以五色彩帛作成冠帶衣服，于門外奠而焚之，
曰送寒衣。

清　富察敦崇《燕京歲時記》

【語譯】

[夏曆]十月初一，普通老百姓的家庭都要祭祖宗掃墓，如中
元節儀式[一般]。傍晚在紙錢上寫上[親人的姓名、輩份]，[像寄
家信一樣]，連同用彩綢做成的帽子、帶子和衣服，在家門外祭奠
後燒掉，這稱為"送寒衣"。

【註釋】

1. 送寒衣：也稱"燒衣節"，流行於全國大多數地區的祭祀習俗。夏曆十
　 月天氣漸冷，人們認為要為死去在陰間中的親人送衣取暖，故有此
　 俗。
2. 士民：指士大夫和普通老百姓。

50 Sending Clothes for the Winter[1]

On the first day of the tenth lunar month, families offer sacrifices to ancestors and sweep the tombs much as they do in the Zhong Yuan Festival[2]. In the evening, they write the names and ranks of their ancestors on paper money (as if they were sending out letters) and offer it as a sacrifice along with hats and clothes made of colourful silks. They burn these things outside their houses after a sacrificial ceremony. This custom is called "sending clothes for the winter".

Fucha Duncong (Qing Dynasty):
Annual Records of the Capital

Notes:

1. Sending clothes for the winter: also called "Clothes-burning Festival", is a sacrificial custom observed in most parts of China. Weather starts to become cold in October of the lunar year, so people think it is time to send clothes to their kin in the nether world. The custom was thus established.

2. Zhong Yuan Festival: see Passage 51.

五十一　中元節[1]祭祀亡靈

七月十五中元節。先數日，市井賣冥器[2]靴鞋、襆頭帽子、金犀假帶[3]、五彩衣服。……又以竹竿斫成三腳，高三五尺，上織燈窩之狀，謂之盂蘭盆，掛搭衣服冥錢[4]在上焚之。構肆樂人，自過七夕，便般《目連救母》[5]雜劇，直至十五日止，觀者增倍。……十五日供養祖先素食。……城外有新墳者，即往拜掃。

宋　孟元老《東京夢華錄》

【語譯】

[夏曆] 七月十五是中元節。這之前的幾天，市上 [開始] 賣紙做的鞋類、帽類、衣帶類物品和五彩的衣服 [供焚化給死者用]。[人們] 還把竹竿削成三腳架，高達三五尺，上方編成類似燈碗形狀，稱它為"盂蘭盆"，紙衣、冥錢就是掛放在這上面燒掉的。戲院裏的演員過了七月初七就開始演出雜劇《目連救母》，直到十五日為止，觀眾 [比平時] 多一倍。十五日 [這天要] 用素食供奉祖先。城外有新墳的人家，[在這天] 也去 [那兒] 祭掃。

51 Offering Sacrifices to Ghosts in Zhong Yuan Festival[1]

The fifteenth day of the seventh lunar month is the Zhong Yuan Festival. Several days ahead of this date, people start to market boots and shoes, hats and belts, and colourful clothes, all made of paper. These items will be burnt as offerings to ghosts . They also make bamboo tripods three to five feet tall, the top part of which is in the shape of a lamp bowl. This is called the *"yu lan* pot". The paper garments and paper money are burnt in it. Operatic troupes put on the play "Mu Lian Rescuing His Mother"[2] from the 7th till the 15th. The audience in that period is double the usual size. On the fifteenth day of the month, people offer vegetarian food to their ancestors. Any family that has a new tomb outside the town must pay homage to it on that day.

Meng Yuanlao (Song Dynasty):
Records of Dreams in East Capital

【註釋】

1. 中元節：也稱"盂蘭盆節"、"鬼節"。祭祀先人亡魂是節日的主要內容。祭祀完畢，焚化紙衣紙錢是節日的高潮。由於盂蘭盆這種竹製的三腳盛物本身也被燒掉，所以這種祭祀儀式叫"盂蘭盆會"。

2. 冥器：焚化給死人的器物，用紙做成。

3. 濮頭帽子、金犀假帶：濮頭是宋代的一種帶有左右兩翅的官帽。金犀，指黃金和犀牛角，常用作裝飾。官帽、官袍帶為普通人禁用的服飾，然而民間習俗中，生前是平民的死者，他的冥器卻可包括紙做的官帽、官袍帶。

4. 冥錢：給死者用的錢幣。

5. 目連救母：佛經說，佛祖的弟子目蓮曾設百味果，供養十方僧人，解救在極度困苦中的母親。舊時民間習俗，每年七月十五都要演出《目連救母》劇，觀眾如雲。

Notes:

1. Zhong Yuan Festival: i.e., Yu Lan Pot Festival, or Ghost Festival, is celebrated mainly to offer sacrifices to the souls of deceased people. The climax is the burning of paper garments and paper money. Since the *yu lan* pot itself is also burnt at the end, the sacrificial rite is called the Yu Lan Pot Fair.

2. "Mu Lian Rescuing His Mother": According to Buddhist scriptures, the Buddhist disciple Mu Lian once furnished monks with all kinds of fruit to secure his mother's rescue from privation. It was a custom in the old times to perform the play on July 15th of the lunar year. The audience crowded the theatre on that day.

五十二　掃晴娘[1] 止雨

雨久，以白紙作婦人首，剪紅綠紙衣之，以苕帚苗縛小帚，令攜之，竿懸檐際，曰掃晴娘。

明　劉侗　于奕正《帝京景物略》

【語譯】

下雨時間太長，[民間]用白紙作成女人的頭，剪紅色和綠色的紙為衣服，用苕帚絲綁一個小掃帚，讓[紙女人]拿着，[把它繫在]竹竿上掛在屋檐下，稱[她]為"掃晴娘"。

【註釋】

1. 掃晴娘：天氣久雨不止，民間女子就用紙做一女人，攜着小掃帚，掛在屋簷下祈求天晴。有的地方稱作"掃天婆"。此習俗流行於北京、陝西和江蘇等地區。

52 The *Sao Qing* Girl[1] Stopping the Rain

If it rains incessantly, people make a woman's head out of white paper and dress it up in clothes made of red and green paper. They attach a small broom made of whiskbroom straw to this doll and tie it to a bamboo pole. Then they hang the pole under the eaves. The paper woman is called the *sao qing* (sweeping to brightness) girl.

Liu Tong and Yu Yizheng (Ming Dynasty):
Scenery and Events in the Capital

Notes:

1. The *sao qing* Girl: In times of incessant rain, the folk women will make a paper woman and hang it up under the eaves to pray for good weather. In some places, this paper woman is called the *sao qing* girl.

五十三 桃木驅邪

桃木辛氣惡，故能壓服邪氣，今人門上用桃符[1]避邪
以此也。

明　李時珍《本草綱目》

帖畫雞戶上，懸葦索于其上，插桃符其傍，百鬼畏
之。按：……《括地圖》曰：“桃都山有大桃樹，盤曲三
千里，上有金雞，日照則鳴。下有兩神，一名鬱，一名
壘，并執葦以伺不祥之鬼，得則殺之。”

南朝梁　宗懍《荊楚歲時記》

【語譯】

桃木有濃烈的刺激氣味，所以能壓服邪氣，現在人的家門上
懸掛桃符避邪就是這個原因。

在紙帖上畫隻雞，貼在門上，把葦草編成的繩狀物懸掛在雞
畫的上面，桃符立在雞畫的兩旁。各種鬼都會害怕。按語：……
《括地圖》[這本書上]説：“桃都山上有棵大桃樹，盤旋彎曲三千
里，樹上有隻金雞，太陽照在樹上，金雞就叫了。桃樹下有兩個
神，一個名叫鬱，一個名叫壘，[他們]手中拿着葦草做的繩索觀
察守候着作惡的鬼，抓到了，就把它殺死。”

53   Peachwood to Repel Evil Influence

Peachwood has a strong irritating smell. Thus, it can suppress evil influences. This is the reason why people put up *tao fu*[1] on their doors.

Li Shizheng (Ming Dynasty):
A Compendium of Materia Medica

Put up the portrait of a chicken on the door, hang a reed rope on top of it, place two pieces of *tao fu* beside it, and all ghosts will be afraid. According to Kuo Ditu, "There is a big peach tree in Taodu Mountain. Its twining branches and roots measure a thousand miles. A golden chicken on this tree crows when the sun rises. Two gods guarding under the tree, named Yu and Lei, await evil ghosts with reed ropes in their hands. When they catch one, they kill it."

Zong Lin (Southern Dynasties, the State of Liang):
Stories of the Jing and Chu Times

【註釋】

1. 桃符：夏曆新年時民間喜用的一種門飾，用桃木板做成，上面畫着兩個門神，借以驅鬼避邪。明代以後改用紙。

Notes:

1. *tao fu*: a kind of decoration on the door commonly used during the Lunar New Year. It is made of peachwood plaques painted with the images of two door gods. People use these talismans to drive away ghosts and repel evil influences. Since the Ming Dynasty, they have been made of paper instead.

五十四　翻經轉男身

六日故事[1]，人家曝書籍圖畫于庭，云蠹魚不生。……是日，諸叢林各以藏經曝烈日中，僧人集村嫗為翻經會，謂翻經十次，他生可轉男身。

清　顧祿《清嘉錄》

【語譯】

[夏曆六月]初六，照舊時的習俗，[民間]家庭把書籍、圖畫放在庭院中曝曬，據說這樣不會生蛀蟲。這天，各個大寺院都把收藏的佛經放在烈日下去曝曬。和尚召集老年的村姑舉行"翻經會"，據說[她們只要]翻動佛經十次，下一世就能轉做男人。

【註釋】

1. 故事：舊時的規定、習慣。

54 Leafing through Scriptures to Be Transformed into Males

It is an old custom for households to dry their collection of books and paintings in their yards under the strong sun on the sixth day of the sixth lunar month. It is believed that by doing so, no bookworms would infest the books and paintings. On that day, temples dry their scriptures in the sun and monks organize Scripture Leafing Sodalities among the old village women, who believe that if they leaf through the scriptures ten times, they could be transformed into males in their next incarnation.

Gu Lu (Qing Dynasty):
Worthy Records of the Qing Dynasty

五十五　石敢當[1]

今人家正門適當巷陌橋道之衝，則立一小石將軍或植一小石碑，鐫其上曰“石敢當”，以厭禳之。按：西漢史游《急就章》云“石敢當。”顏師古註曰：“……敢當，所向無敵也。”據所說，則世之用此，亦欲以為保障之意。

明　陶宗儀《南村輟耕錄》

【語譯】

當今人家的大門正好對着巷口大路橋頭等要道處，常立一個石雕的武士像或豎一塊小石碑，在上面刻着“石敢當”，用來壓禁消除不祥。按語：西漢史游的《急就章》中說到“石敢當”，顏師古註釋說：“……敢當，就是所去的地方，沒有人能阻擋得了。”據這個說法，那麼民間用石敢當，即是希望因有它的保護[而獲得安全]的意思。

【註釋】

1. 石敢當：許多城鎮農村的街巷之口立一塊石片作為禁壓不祥之物，上刻"石敢當"或"泰山石敢當"，這種以石作鎮物的巫術，流行全國很多地方。

55 Stone *Gandang*[1]

Nowadays, a stone statue of a warrior figure or a milestone is usually put in front of a house in a position facing toward streets or bridges. The inscription on it, "Stone *Gandang*", is meant to suppress and dispel inauspicious influences. Stone *Gandang* was originally mentioned in Ji Jiu Zhang in the travel notes written in the West Han Dynasty[2]. Yan Shigu[3] annotated it: "*gandang*, i.e., invincible". According to his notes, people use this practice to seek protection.

Tao Zongyi (Ming Dynasty):
Records of Stopping Farming in South Village

Notes:

1. Stone *Gandang*: A piece of stone is set at the opening of roads in towns and villages with the inscription "Stone *Gandang*" or "Mount Taishan Stone *Gandang*", *gandang* meaning invincible. This fetish is set up in many parts of the country.

2. West Han Dynasty: 206B.C.-25A.D.

3. Yan Shigu: a scholar of the Tang Dynasty (618-907), known for his critical interpretation of classical texts.

五十六　噴嚏兆災 [1]

　　今人噴嚏必唾曰：好人說我常安樂，惡人說我齒牙落。

　　　　　　　　　　　明　李詡《戒庵漫筆》

【語譯】

　　現在人 [如] 打噴嚏一定吐唾沫說：好人在祝福我常常保持平安快樂的生活，惡人在議論我牙齒脫落 [的事]。

【註釋】

1. 噴嚏兆災：民間認為，人偶然打噴嚏是有人在背後議論或有災禍臨頭的徵兆，或是因有人思念所致，此習俗流傳至今。

56   Sneezing Portending Disaster[1]

Now when people sneeze, they spit[2] and say, "Good people are blessing me with a peaceful and happy life; evil people are cursing me with loss of teeth."

Li Qu (Ming Dynasty):
Jottings in Abstinence Hut

Notes:

1. Sneezing portending disaster: It is popularly believed that if a person sneezes, it is because someone is gossiping behind his back or it is an ill omen. Yet some believe it is because someone is missing him.

2. spit: Sneezing is supposed to forebode bad luck, just as is mistakenly saying something taboo or inauspicious. To undo the harm, some folk have the custom of spitting as a symbol of counteracting the ominous sneezing or the previous remark, and say something auspicious anew instead.

五十七　忌帶綠頭巾[1]

　　娼妓有不隸于官，家居賣姦者，謂之土妓。俗謂之私
窠子。又以妻之外淫者，目其夫為烏龜，蓋龜不能交，縱
牝者與蛇交也……國初之制，綠其巾以示辱，蓋古赭衣[2]
之意。至今里門，尚以綠頭巾相戲也。

清　翟灝《通俗篇》

【語譯】

　　[如有] 娼妓未在官府註冊，而在自己家裏賣淫的，被稱為土
妓，俗稱為"私窠子"。民間又將妻子在外面淫亂 [這樣的] 事，而
把她的丈夫看作烏龜，[這是因為]，烏龜不能交配，縱容雌龜和蛇
交媾。[清代] 初年規定，把這種丈夫的頭巾染綠表示他受到了污
辱，就像古代穿赭色囚衣那樣的意思。直到今天鄉里還用綠頭巾
[與別人] 開玩笑呢。

【註釋】

1. 綠頭巾：民間以綠頭巾 (或綠帽子) 羞辱妻子在外淫亂的男人。作為服
　　飾禁忌，至今流傳全國。
2. 赭衣：古代囚犯所穿的暗紅色的衣服。也作為囚犯的代稱。

57　Green Scarf Taboo[1]

If a prostitute does business at home instead of in a government licenced brothel, she is called a "home prostitute", or locally, a "private nest". If someone's wife is licentious, he is called a "tortoise". Probably this is because a male tortoise cannot mate and has to connive at the female's mating with a snake. It was a regulation in the early years of the Qing Dynasty that the scarves of such cuckolds be dyed green to display their disgrace. This practice is just like wearing dark red clothes[2] in ancient times. Up to this day, people still tease others by saying that they wear green scarves.

Zhai Hao (Qing Dynasty):
Articles on Popular Things

Notes:

1. Green scarf taboo: People label those whose wives are adulterous as wearing green scarves or green hats. Thus, green scarves or green hats are taboo in China.

2. wearing dark red clothes: Dark red clothes were worn by prisoners in ancient times. It has become a metonymy for prisoners.

五十八　蠶禁[1]

　　環太湖諸山，鄉人比戶蠶桑為務。三四月為蠶月，紅紙黏門，不相往來，多所禁忌。治其事者，自陌上桑柔，提籠採葉，至村中繭煮，分箔繅絲，歷一月，而後馳諸禁。

清　顧祿《清嘉錄》

【語譯】

　　環繞太湖的各座山中，鄉下人家家戶戶以養蠶種桑樹為業。[夏曆] 三、四月是蠶月，[各家人家] 把紅紙黏在門上，相互間不往來，很多事都有禁忌。專做養蠶工作的人，從田間桑樹上 [出現] 柔軟的葉子 [開始]，提着竹籃採桑葉，到村中煮蠶繭，在竹篩子上繅絲，歷時一個月，然後才解除各種禁忌。

【註釋】

1. 蠶禁：蠶月的禁忌。流行江蘇、浙江杭嘉湖地區。

58 Silkworm Taboo[1]

In the mountains that surround the Tai Hu Lake, village people live by planting mulberry trees and raising silkworms. A month of abstinence assuring bountiful silk harvests runs from the middle of the third lunar month to the middle of the fourth. People put red paper on their doors and avoid visiting one another. Many other things are prohibited. In this season, silkworm farmers start working as soon as the soft mulberry leaves appear in the groves. They carry baskets to pick the leaves, boil silkworm cocoons in the village and reel silk in bamboo sieves. These jobs last for a month. Afterwards the taboos are lifted.

Gu Lu (Qing Dynasty):
Worthy Records of the Qing Dynasty

Notes:

1. Silkworm taboo: taboo observed in the silkworm month in Jiangsu Province and the Hangjiahu area in Zhejiang Province.

五十九　看骨相[1]

　　唐貞元末，有相骨山人[2]，瞽雙目，人求相，以手捫之，必知貴賤。房次卿……訪之，及出戶時，後謁者盈巷。睹次卿已出，迎問之曰："如何。"答曰："不足言。不足言。且道個瘦長杜秀才位及人臣，何必更云。"後杜循果帶印鎮西蜀也。

宋《太平廣記》卷七十六引《嘉語錄》

【語譯】

　　唐代貞元末年，有一個會看骨相的山人，雙眼失明，有人求他看相，他 [只] 用手摸摸此人，就必定能預言其貴賤禍福了。房次卿去訪問他，等到房次卿走出他家門時，後面 [欲] 求進見的人把巷子都擠滿了。看見房次卿已出來，都迎上前去問他："怎麼樣？"房次卿回答說："不值得談，不值得談。他尚且說那個又瘦又長的杜秀才有大臣 [那麼] 高的地位，還有甚麼必要再說呢！"[不料] 後來杜循果然帶着官印 [作了] 鎮守西蜀 [的大官]。

【註釋】

1.　看骨相：根據人的骨骼情況來判斷人的命運好壞。民間的占卜方式之一。

2.　山人：指從事卜卦、算命等職業的人。

59 Reading Bone Structure[1]

In the late Zhen Yuan period of the Tang Dynasty (805), there was a blind fortune-teller who could read people's fortune from their bone structure. If people asked to have their fortunes told, he would touch them with his hands and be able to accurately predict their fortunes or misfortunes. Fang Ciqing went to visit him. By the time he left, other inquirers had already jammed the lane. Seeing him come out, they asked, "How was it?" Fang replied, "Not worth mentioning. He went so far as to say that the reedy *xiucai*[2] Du would become a government minister. What else can I say?" Later, Du was given the royal seal and became the governor of West Shu.

(Song Dynasty): Tai Ping Guang Ji (Book 76)

Notes:

1. Reading bone structure: telling the destiny of people by reading their bone structure, one of the means of divination practised among common people.

2. *xiucai*: one who passed the imperial examination at the court level in the Ming and Qing Dynasties.

六十　儺舞驅疫[1]

　　儺之為名，著于時令矣。自宮禁至于下俚，皆得以逐災邪而驅疫癘。故都會惡少年則以是時鳥獸其形容，皮革其面目。

唐　羅隱《市儺》

【語譯】

　　儺的聲名，是與歲時節聯繫在一起的。從宮廷到民間，都認為跳儺舞可趕走災難邪祟驅除瘟疫。因此城裏調皮的年輕人就把那個時令的鳥獸的樣子〔畫在儺舞者的面具上〕，假面具是用皮革做成的。

【註釋】

1. 儺舞：古代舉行驅除疫鬼時的舞蹈。跳儺舞的人戴着面具，或者直接在臉上塗畫，手持干戈等兵器，大多以表演驅鬼趕鬼為內容。後在長期的發展中出現表現勞動生活和民間傳說為內容的節目。個別地區由儺舞發展成戲曲的形式，稱為"儺戲"。

60 *Nuo* Dancing[1] to Dispel Epidemic Diseases

The *Nuo* Dance was closely related to the seasons. From the imperial court to the folk, it was believed that the dance could dispel epidemic diseases and disastrous evils. While dancing, rowdy youths in big cities wore leather masks patterned on seasonable birds and beasts.

Luo Yin (Tang Dynasty):
Scenes of Nuo Dancing

Notes:

1. *Nuo* Dance: a kind of dance to dispel epidemic diseases in ancient times. Holding weapons of war dancers wore masks or painted their faces. The main contents of the dance were performances to drive away evil spirits. Throughout the years this dance has evolved to manifest many aspects of folk work and life.

六十一　月光紙[1]

　　紙肆市月光紙，繢滿月像，趺坐蓮華者，月光徧照菩薩也。華下月輪桂殿，有兔杵而人立，搗藥臼中。紙小者三寸，大者丈，緻工者金碧繽紛。家設月光位于月所出方，向月供而拜，則焚月光紙撤所供，散家之人必徧。

　　　　　　　　明　劉侗　于奕正《帝京景物略》

【語譯】

　　紙店賣月光紙，繪滿月的圖像，盤腿坐在蓮花上的是月光遍照菩薩。花下的月宮中，有個兔子 [拿着] 棒槌如人般站立着，在 [玉] 臼中搗藥。小型的月光紙三寸，大型的高一丈，製做得金碧輝煌，五彩繽紛。[民間] 家庭把月光菩薩的座位安排在月亮出來的方向，對着月奉上供品並祭拜，結束時燒去月光紙，撤下的供品必須分送給家中的每一個人。

【註釋】

1. 月光紙：繪有月神和月宮的紙。民間在中秋節時祭月用。
2. 月輪桂殿：指月宮。滿月是輪狀的；又傳說月亮中有神奇的桂花樹，故稱月宮"桂殿"。

61   Moonlight Paper[1]

Moonlight paper is sold at stationers. On the paper there are two representations: the full moon and the Moonlight Buddha sitting cross-legged on the lotus seat. In the first of these, the moon (under a canopy of flowers) contains the Laurel Palace[2] in which a rabbit stands pounding medicine with a pestle in a jade mortar. Small versions of the moonlight paper are about ten centimetres long. Big ones are three metres high. They are of excellent craftsmanship, resplendent and magnificent. Families put the Moonlight Buddha in the direction of the rising moon. They offer sacrifices and make obeisance to the moon. When the ceremony is over, the moonlight paper is burnt and the offerings, cleared away, are distributed to every member of the family.

Liu Tong and Yu Yizheng (Ming Dynasty):
Scenery and Events in the Capital

Notes:

1. Moonlight paper: a piece of paper with paintings of the moon god and the moon palace. It was used at the ceremony of offering sacrifices to the moon during the Mid-Autumn Festival.

2. Laurel Palace: Legends have it that a miracle laurel tree stands beside the moon palace which is thus called the Laurel Palace.

六十二　祈子摩睺羅[1]

　　七月七夕……賣磨喝樂，乃小塑土偶耳。悉以雕木彩
裝欄座，或用碧紗籠，或飾以金珠牙翠，有一對直數千
者。……又小兒須買新荷葉執之，蓋效顰磨喝樂，兒童輩
特地新妝，競誇鮮麗。……磨喝樂本佛經摩睺羅，今通俗
而書之。

宋　孟元老《東京夢華錄》

　　京語謂之摩睺羅，大小甚不一，價也不廉，或加飾以
男女衣服，有及于華奢，南人目為巧兒。

宋　金盈之《新編醉翁談錄》

【語譯】

　　七月初七，[街上] 賣磨喝樂，這是一種小型的用泥土塑成的
人像。[人們] 用彩色的木雕裝飾它座像的欄圍，有的用綠紗罩
著，有的飾以金子、珍珠、象牙和翡翠，有一對價值 [貴至] 數千
的。小孩都要把買來的新鮮荷葉拿在手裏，這是在效仿磨喝樂的
樣子啊。兒童都特別地穿上新的衣服，互相比賽及誇耀自己服飾
的鮮艷美麗。磨喝樂 [的名字] 來源於佛經中的摩睺羅，現在的人

62   Praying for a Son from *Mohouluo*[1]

On the seventh day of the seventh lunar month merchants sell *mohele* — a kind of small clay figurine. People decorate its plinth with colourful wood carvings. Some of these figurines are enveloped in jade-coloured gauze; some are decorated with gold, pearls, ivory or jadeite. A pair of these decorated *mohele* can be worth as much as several thousand dollars. Children mimic the postures of these figurines, clasping fresh lotus leaves bought for the purpose, and compete in such imitations in their fancy clothes. The name *mohele* was taken from Buddha Mohouluo, a personage in Buddhist scriptures, and these statues are now commonly called *mohele*.

> *Meng Yuanlao (Song Dynasty):*
> *Records of Dreams in East Capital*

People in the capital call them *mohouluo*. They vary in size, but are all expensive. Some are dressed as boys and girls and are flamboyantly decorated. Southerners call these figures *qiaoer* — artsy kids.

> *Jin Yingzhi (Song Dynasty):*
> *New Edition of Babblings of a Drunkard*

通俗寫成磨喝樂。

　　京城話稱為摩喉羅 [的塑像] ，大小不都一樣，價格也不便宜。有的 [身上] 還穿上了男女服裝，某些 [摩喉羅的裝飾] 到了華麗奢侈的地步。南方人稱它為巧兒。

【註釋】

1. 摩喉羅：也稱磨喝樂、摩侯羅。民間泥木製作的玩具娃娃，流行於中原和江南地區。摩喉羅原為佛經中的一位神的名稱。唐代婦女用蠟做成嬰兒的形狀，將其浮於水上作祈子的遊戲，稱它為摩喉羅。至宋代即演變為七夕市場上專賣的土偶或木偶，象徵祈子。

Notes:

1. *Mohouluo*: also named *mohele*, is a kind of clay doll made by people in the middle and southern parts of China. *Mohouluo* is the name of a Buddha in the Buddhist scriptures. Women in the Tang Dynasty carved wax figures of babies and floated them on water to beg for babies. These figures were called *mohouluo* then. In the Song Dynasty it was a custom to sell clay or wooden dolls in the market on the Double Seventh Day, used as a symbol of praying for children.

六十三　沏茶待客[1]

茶見于唐時，味苦而轉甘，晚採者為茗[2]。……今世俗，客至則啜茶，……此俗遍天下。

宋　朱彧《萍州可談》

客至則設茶，欲去則設湯[3]，不知起于何時。然上自官府，下至閭里，莫之或廢。

宋　佚名《南窗紀談》

【語譯】

茶在唐代時就常見了，[它的]味道[開始喝是有些]苦而後轉為甜，晚採的茶叫"茗"。現在普通人家，客人到了就[請他]喝茶，[可見]這種習俗已經傳遍天下了。

客人到了[給他]泡茶，客人將要離去[時給他]送[一碗]湯，[這種習俗]不知從甚麼時候開始的。但是上自官府，下至普通老百姓[家]，[始終]沒有廢除。

63   Making Tea for Guests[1]

Tea has been popular since the Tang Dynasty. It tastes bitter at first and then turns sweet. Tea leaves that are picked late are called *ming*[2]. Ordinary families offer a guest tea on his arrival. This has now become a well-observed practice.

Zhu Yu (Song Dynasty):
Good Talks of Pingzhou

Upon the arrival of a guest, tea is prepared; at his departure, soup[3] is proffered. The origin of these practices cannot be traced. At any rate, this custom has never been abandoned either at the government level or in ordinary households.

Anonymous (Song Dynasty):
Chronicles Written by a South Window

【註釋】

1. 沏茶待客：此習俗從南北朝起開始，流傳至今，是中國人最普通最常見的交際習俗。

2. 茗：古時將晚收的茶叫作"茗"，後來"茗"也用以泛指茶。

3. 設湯：此種湯是用甘草等香甜的藥材碎屑熬成的。最初"設湯"僅是送客的禮節，到後來卻成了逐客的方式。然用以逐客的習俗現已不存在。

Notes:

1. Making tea for guests: This custom started in the Northern and Southern Dynasties (420-589). Even now, it is popularly practised.

2. *ming*: In ancient times, tea leaves picked late were called *ming*. Now, *ming* is used as a general term for tea.

3. soup: This is a soup made by boiling sweet-tasting herbs like licorice root. Originally, soup was offered as a gesture of courtesy at the departure of a guest, but later it was offered as a hint that the visit should draw to a close. Now this custom no longer exists.

六十四　下茶為禮[1]

茶不移本，植必生子。古人結婚，必以茶為禮，取其
不移植之意也。

明　郎瑛《七修類編》

【語譯】

茶樹的根是不能移動的，種植了茶樹[它]一定結籽。古代人
結婚必定用茶葉作為[訂親的]禮品，[就是]取它不能移植[他處，
具有堅定不變的品性]的意思。

【註釋】

1. 下茶為禮：將茶葉作訂親的禮品，此習俗流傳至今。某些人家訂親的
   聘禮中雖無茶葉，可仍叫作"下茶"，或叫"茶禮"，表示決不改易之
   意。

174

64   Sending Tea as a Gift[1]

Tea bushes cannot be transplanted, but once planted they are sure to produce seeds. In olden days, therefore, when people got married, they would be sent tea as a betrothal gift, in reference to the plant's steadfastness.

Lang Ying (Ming Dynasty):
Qi Xiu Lei Bian

Notes:

1. Sending tea as a gift: The custom of making tea a betrothal gift is still practised. Sometimes, although tea is not included, the gift is still called a "tea gift", signifying fidelity.

六十五　上茶館

　　京師茶館，列長案，茶葉與水之資，須分計之；有提壺以往者，可自備茶葉，出錢買水而已。……八旗[1]人士，雖官至三四品[2]，也廁身其間，並提鳥籠，曳長裾，就廣坐，作茗憩，與圉人走卒[3]雜坐談話，不以為忤也。然絕無權要中人之蹤迹。

徐珂《清稗類鈔》

【語譯】

　　京城(指北京)的茶館中排放着長條桌子，茶葉的價錢和水的價錢是須分開來計算的。提着自己的茶壺去[那兒]的人，可以自帶茶葉，[只]出錢買水就行了。滿族人，雖然官位達三品四品，也參與其間，還提着鳥籠，拖着長袖，在普通的位子上坐下，喝茶休憩，和養馬人、差役等混坐在一起談話，[也]不認為是違背[禮節]的。但是[茶館中]絕對沒有高官權要之人的蹤迹。

【註釋】

1. 八旗：清代滿族的軍隊和戶口編制，以八種旗為標誌。
2. 三四品：古代官吏的等級分為九品，三、四品官員屬中級。
3. 圉人走卒：養馬的人和差役。這兒泛指社會地位低下，供人差遣的人。

65   Going to a Teahouse

Teahouses in the capital (i.e. Beijing) featured long tables. At these teahouses guests were charged separately for the tea leaves and the hot water, so that if you wished you could bring your own teapot and tea leaves and pay only for the water. There, one could even see officials of the third and fourth ranks[1] with their caged birds and wearing long sleeves, sitting among the common people. Sipping tea, they relaxed and chatted with horseherders and government lackeys, and no one felt they were violating social etiqutte. But of course you would see neither hide nor hair of VIPs or high officials in these teahouses.

Xu Ke : Classified Anecdotes of the Qing Dynasty

Notes:

1. the third and fourth ranks: In ancient China, officials were classified into nine ranks, the first rank being the highest. So third and fourth ranks were around the middle in the echelon.

六十六 茶肆[1]景觀

插四時花，掛名人畫，裝點門面。四時賣奇茶異湯……敲打響盞歌賣，止用瓷盞漆托供賣，則無銀盂物也。……大凡茶樓多有富室子弟、諸司下直等人會聚，習學樂器、上教曲賺之類，謂之"掛牌兒"。……亦有諸行借工賣伎人會聚行老[2]，謂之"市頭"。大街有三五家開茶肆，樓上專安着妓女，名曰"花茶坊"。……非君子駐足之地也。更有張賣麵店隔壁黃尖嘴蹴球茶坊，……蔣檢閱茶肆，皆士大夫期朋約友會聚之處。

宋　吳自牧《夢粱錄》

【語譯】

[杭州城裏的茶坊裏]插着四季的鮮花，掛着名人的畫，用以裝飾門面。[按照]四季的[變化]經營[各種不同的]特色茶水和湯類。[夥計]敲打着茶盞響亮地歌唱叫賣，[通常]只使用瓷的茶盞和漆器的茶托子，沒有銀製的小碗等器皿。一般茶樓大多有富裕人家的年輕人、各官署當值結束的人聚會一起，作學習樂器、練習說唱曲目一類[的活動]，這稱作"掛牌兒"。也有欲招工匠的人和有專業特長的匠人為找工做的，[在茶坊中]與各行業的頭兒聚會[請他作介紹]，這稱作"市頭"。大街上有幾家茶坊的樓上安

66　Scenes of Famous Teahouses[1]

Teahouses displayed seasonal flowers and famous paintings. Different seasons called forth exotic teas and special soups. Rather than silver service one could see only china teacups and lacquerware trays. In general, teahouses served as places where young men from rich families and off-duty government officials gathered to learn to play musical instruments and practise numbers from local operas. Teahouses of this kind were called "hung-out-shingle" places. Other teahouses where craftsmen seeking a job met guild masters were called "hiring halls". Teahouses accommodating prostitutes on the upper floor were called "flower teahouses". They were not the kind of place a man of moral integrity set foot on. Ordinary teahouses with names like Caustic-tongued Huang's Ball-kicking Teahouse Next to Zhang's Noodle Shop and Jiang Jianyue's Teahouse were places where government officials and scholars met their friends.

Wu Zimu (Song Dynasty):
Records of a Pipe Dream

置着妓女，這種茶坊名叫"花茶坊"。這不是正派人逗留的地方啊。再有張賣麵店隔壁的黃尖嘴踢球茶坊……及蔣檢閱茶坊等，都是官僚階層和有聲望的讀書人與朋友約會聚首的地方。

【註釋】

1. 茶肆：即賣茶的店子，也叫茶坊、茶樓、茶館。南宋首都臨安（今杭州）的茶坊依據顧客的特點分成好幾類，當時各階層人士都喜歡上茶肆，茶館佈置得十分講究，使得茶客願意在那兒久留。
2. 行老：古代大都市裏各行各業的頭兒，兼為他人介紹職業。

Notes:

1. teahouses: places where the tea-loving Chinese enjoy drinking tea and meet and chat with their friends by the way. They are like cafés in the Western countries where people meet for social exchanges.

六十七　猜拳[1]

　　大凡放令[2]，欲端其頸如一枝孤柏，澄其神如萬里長江，揚其膺如猛虎蹲踞，運其眸如烈日飛動，差其指如鷥欲翔舞，柔其腕如龍欲蜿蜒。

唐　皇甫崧《醉鄉日月》

【語譯】

　　通常[在酒席上]猜拳[的人]，他的頸子擺出[的姿勢]就像一棵孤枝獨立的柏樹，他的神態就變成像萬里長江般的清澄[專注]，他像蹲踞著的猛虎[那樣]挺起了胸脯，轉動他的雙眼好像火樣的太陽在飛動，他的手指變幻無窮就像鷥鳥飛翔起舞，他的手腕如同蟠龍蜿蜒游動時似的柔軟。

【註釋】

1. 猜拳：也稱"拇戰"。酒席上的助興遊戲，方法多種。此習俗至今流行於全國各地。
2. 放令：即猜拳。古代人稱手勢酒令。

67   Finger-Guessing Game[1]

When a drinker plays the finger-guessing game, his neck sticks out like a lone cypress. His look becomes as serious and focused as the Yangtze River. He throws out his chest like a prancing tiger. His eyeballs rotate like a fiery sun. His fingers flutter like flying birds. His wrists slither smoothly like coiling dragons.

Huangfu Song (Tang Dynasty):
Days and Nights in Drunkland

Notes:

1. Finger-guessing game: an entertainment during a banquet in which players guess the fingers they show in turn and the loser will have to drink up his cup of wine.

六十八 金蘭會[1]

廣州順德村落女子，多以拜盟結姐妹，名金蘭會。女
出嫁後歸寧，恆不返夫家，至有未成夫妻禮，必俟同盟姐
妹嫁畢，然後各返夫家。若促之過甚，則眾姐妹相約自
盡。

清　梁紹壬《兩般秋雨庵隨筆》

【語譯】

廣州順德那兒的農村婦女，大多數結成異姓的姐妹，名叫
"金蘭會"。姑娘出嫁後 [即] 回娘家，長久地不回夫家，甚至還有
未曾和丈夫同房的。她們一定要等異姓的姐妹全都出嫁了，然後
才各自返回丈夫家。如果催促她們 [回去] 太急，那麼這些姐妹們
就會相互約好一起自殺。

【註釋】

1. 金蘭會：一種終身不結婚的婦女組織。會中婦女之間情感勝似姐妹，
   猶如夫婦。

68   Gold Orchid Sororities[1]

The village girls in Shunde, Guangzhou tend to form sisterhoods under the name of "gold orchid sororities". Soon after they marry, they go back to live with their parents, and do not return to their husbands for extended durations. Some do not even spend a single night with their husbands. They commit themselves to returning to their husbands only when all the sorority members are married. They pledge that if they are forced to return they will commit mass suicide.

Liang Shaoren (Qing Dynasty):
Jottings in "Autumn Rain Hut of a Different Kind"

Notes:

1. Gold Orchid Sororities: Women in these groups develop attachments, closer than sisters', almost like husbands and wives.

六十九　鬥蟋蟀[1]

祭甫訖，輒于墓次掏促織，滿袋則喜，秌桿肩之以
歸。是月始鬥促織，壯夫士人亦為之。鬥有場，場有主
者，其養之又有師，斗盆筒罐，無家不貯焉。

明　劉侗　于奕正《帝京景物略》

【語譯】

祭祀剛完，[人們] 就在墓邊上掏捉蟋蟀，口袋裝滿了，很高
興，用高粱桿扛着蟋蟀回家。從這個月 [夏曆七月] 開始鬥蟋蟀，
體力勞動者和讀書人全都參加。鬥蟋蟀有 [專門的] 場地，這場地
有人 [專門] 負責經營，他的蟋蟀又有 [專門的] 師傅 [馴] 養。每
家每戶的斗筲、瓦盆、竹筒或罐子裏都放着蟋蟀。

【註釋】

1. 鬥蟋蟀：每年秋天進行的民間娛樂活動，相傳始於唐代，流行至今。
   舊時各地還開有鬥蟋蟀的賭場，供人以鬥蟋蟀為戲進行賭博。

69 Cricketfight[1]

Once the season for ancestral worship is over, people start catching crickets in cemeteries. Delighted with full bags, they sling their catch over their shoulders on sorghum stalks and swagger home. Cricketfighting starts in the seventh lunar month. Labourers as well as intellectuals gather at special pits for the game run by proprietors. Here they field their professionally trained crickets. During the season, every family garners crickets in bamboo containers, clay pots, bamboo cylinders and jars.

Liu Tong and Yu Yizheng (Ming Dynasty):
Scenery and Events in the Capital

Notes:

1. Cricketfight: a folk entertainment activity popular in autumn. It is said that the custom started in the Tang Dynasty and it still persists. Formerly, there were cricketfighting pits where people gambled on the game.

七十　放風箏[1]

　　風箏盛於清明，其聲在弓，其力在尾；大者方丈，尾長有至二三丈[2]者。式多長方，呼為“板門”；餘以螃蟹、蜈蚣、蝴蝶、蜻蜓、福字、壽字為多。……巧極人工。晚或繫燈于尾，多至連三連五。

　　　　　　　　　　清　李斗《揚州畫舫錄》

【語譯】

　　清明的時候放風箏最為盛行，風箏[嗡嗡的]聲音是[從竹]弓上發出的，它依靠尾部的力量[向上飛翔]。大的[風箏有]一丈見方，尾長有的到二、三丈。大多數的式樣是長方的，這稱作“板門”；其餘的大多是螃蟹、蜈蚣、蝴蝶、蜻蜓、福字、壽字等[式樣]的，手工精巧極了。晚上有的[風箏]的尾部上[還]繫上了小燈，多的[甚至有]連着三個五個燈的。

【註釋】

1. 放風箏：流行於華北、華東、中南地區的民間娛樂活動。風箏用細竹、竹片紮成骨架，糊上棉紙、薄絹製成，玩時用綫牽引，利用風力放上天空。有的地方春日放風箏，有剪斷繩綫，讓其飄走的習俗，據說因此可將晦運帶走。

2. 丈：中國的市制長度單位。一丈有十市尺，三市尺為一米，一丈約三米多長。

70   Kite-flying[1]

The custom of kite-flying prevails during the Clear Brightness Festival (around April 5th). The bamboo crossbow of the kite vibrates with a buzz as it rises aloft on the power of its tail. Big kites can be as broad as ten metres square with a tail of eight to ten metres. Most kites have a rectangular shape. The rest are patterned as crabs, centipedes, butterflies and dragonflies, or Chinese characters such as "fortune" or "longevity". All kites are constructed with fine craftsmanship. When flown in the evening, they have lights attached to their tails and some have as many as three to five lights strung together.

Li Dou (Qing Dynasty):
Records in a Gaily-Painted Pleasure Boat in Yangzhou

Notes:

1. Kite-flying: a kind of folk entertainment which prevails in the north, east, and middle-south parts of China. The frame of the kite is made of thin bamboo strips on which tissue paper or thin silk fabric is glued. In some places, kites are flown in spring, and people deliberately cut the string to let the kite go because they believe in this way it will take away bad luck.

七十一　清晨遛鳥 [1]

每晨多城中籠養之徒，攜白翎雀于堤上學黃鸝聲。白翎雀本北方鳥，江南人好之，飼于籠中，一鳥動輒百金。籠之價值，貴者如金餿盆，中鋪沙矸石，令雀在其上鼓翅，謂之"打蓬"。若畫舫中，每懸之于船楣，以此為戲。次則畫眉、黃豆之屬，不可勝數。

清　李斗《揚州畫舫錄》

【語譯】

每天清晨城裏很多用籠養鳥的人，帶着白翎鳥在湖堤上學黃鸝的叫聲。白翎雀本是北方的鳥，江南人喜歡它，飼養在鳥籠中，一隻鳥動不動就價值百金。鳥籠的價值，貴的就像嵌金的盆一樣。籠中間鋪着碎石，讓鳥在這上面舒展拍打翅膀，這稱作"打蓬"。如果是在畫舫中，每每將鳥籠掛在船前的橫木上，[養鳥人]以此作為趣事。次一等的就是畫眉鳥、黃頸鳥之類了，[鳥的品種]多得數不過來。

【註釋】

1. 清晨遛鳥：清晨提着鳥籠出門散步，與友人匯聚在空曠處呼吸新鮮空氣、交談、諦聽鳥鳴，鳥籠多置於高處。此習俗至今流行於全國各地，遛鳥者多為老年男性。

71   Morning Walk with Birds[1]

Hoping their caged white-feathered birds will learn to sing from the orioles on the banks of the lake, many city people take their birdcages out there with them for a morning's airing. Because white-feathered birds are northern birds which are fancied by people in the south, they can sell for a fortune. Their gilded cages, too, can cost as much as a gold tray. On the gravelled bottom of the cage, birds flutter in a motion called *da peng* (beating the canopy). In gaily-painted pleasure boats, birdcages are hung on the rafters to be admired. Thrushes and yellow-necks are second-class birds, but the variety of birds is beyond counting.

Li Dou (Qing Dynasty) :
Records in a Gaily-Painted Pleasure Boat in Yangzhou

Notes:

1. Morning walk with birds: The custom of taking a morning stroll, carrying one's birdcage and placing it high in an open area while one chats with old friends, breathes the fresh air and listens to the birdsongs is practised all over China. "Bird-walkers" are mostly old men.

七十二 上浴室¹

　　以白石為池，方丈餘，間為大小數格：其大者近鑊水熱，為大池，次者為中池，小而水不甚熱者為娃娃池。貯衣之櫃，環而立于廳事者為座箱，在兩旁者為站箱。內通小室，謂之暖房。茶香灑碧之餘，侍者折枝²按摩，備極豪侈。……除夕浴謂之"洗邋遢³"，端午謂之"百草水⁴"。

　　　　　　　　　　　　　　　　清　李斗《揚州畫舫錄》

【語譯】

　　用白石頭砌成池子，一丈多見方[大]，隔成大小幾格：其中大的靠近[燒水]鍋的較熱，是大池，其次的是中池，小而水不太熱的[那格]是娃娃池。放衣服的櫃子，環繞着廳堂一圈豎着的是座箱，在兩邊的是站箱。直通到裏面的小房間，稱作暖房。[浴客]聞着茶香喝完碧綠的茶水之後，[還有]侍者按摩，豪華奢侈到了極點。除夕洗澡稱為"洗邋遢"，端午洗澡稱為"百草水"。

192

72　Going to the Public Bath[1]

The pools are made of white stone. They are over ten square metres in area and divided into several sections. The big ones close to the boiler are the "big pools". Next to them are the "middle pools". Small ones with lukewarm water are the "babies' pools". Lockers standing in a circle against the walls of the hall are called "sitting boxes", and the ones at the sides, "standing boxes". A corridor leads to small chambers which are called "warm rooms". After drinking fragrant green tea, bathers are offered massage service by the waiters. The service is extravagant indeed. A bath on Chinese New Year's Eve is called "cleaning away dirt", and a bath on Dragon Boat Festival Day is called "a hundred herbs ablution"[2].

Li Dou (Qing Dynasty)
Records in a Gaily-Painted Pleasure Boat in Yangzhou

【註釋】

1. 上浴室：吳方言稱"孵混堂"。一種流行至今的都市習俗。都市的浴室有多種等級，以適宜不同層次的人士使用。上浴室對都市裏的一些人來說還含有貿易、休憩和交際的目的。

2. 折枝：即按摩。

3. 邋遢：不乾淨。

4. 百草水：古代端午節有採集百草，用以燒水洗澡的習俗。傳說因此能驅除穢氣。

Notes:

1. Going to the public bath: also called "hatching the public bath" in Wu dialect, is still practised in cities today. Different classes of public baths cater to the needs of different groups. Going to the public bath also serves the purposes of doing business, relaxation and socializing.

2. a hundred herbs ablution: In ancient times, it was a custom to collect all kinds of herbs, boil them and bathe in the decoction. It was believed that by doing so ill fortune could be washed away.

七十三　觀潮 [1]

　　每歲八月內，潮怒于常時，都人自十一日起，便有觀者，至十六、十八日傾城而出，車馬紛紛，十八日最為繁盛，二十日則稍稀矣……自廟子頭 [2] 直至六和塔 [3]，家家樓屋，盡為貴戚內侍等雇賃作看位觀潮。

宋　吳自牧《夢粱錄》

【語譯】

　　每年八月裏，[錢塘江] 的潮水洶湧澎湃超過了平常的時候，城裏人從十一日那天起，就開始來觀潮，到了十六日、十八日，整個城全部都出動了，[道路上] 車、馬絡繹不絕，十八日 [觀潮的場面] 最盛大最熱鬧，二十日人就略稀少些了。從廟子頭起一直到六和塔這一帶凡是有樓房的人家，全都被皇帝的親屬及宦官等人所租賃作為看位觀潮用。

【註釋】

1. 觀潮：每年夏曆八月十八，浙江錢塘江有大海潮，洪濤高浪，排山而至。杭州地區民間觀錢塘潮習俗自宋代起，至今仍然盛行。
2. 廟子頭：地名。
3. 六和塔：錢塘江邊的一座著名木塔。

73   Watching the Tide[1]

The tides rolling up the Qiantang River surge to their highest in the eighth lunar month. Starting on the 11th, city people come down to watch the flood tide. Between the 11th and the 18th, almost the entire city comes out. Crowds and carriages jam the streets. The spectacle reaches a climax on the 18th. Houses of two or more storeys between Miaozitou[2] and Liuhe Tower[3] are rented by goverment officials and relatives of the emperor as galleries to watch the tide.

Wu Zimu (Song Dynasty):
Records of a Pipe Dream

Notes:

1. Watching the tide: On August 18th of the lunar year, there is a flood tide on the Qiantang River. Turbulent surges and huge waves come like mountains. The custom of residents in the area of Hangzhou watching the tide was established in the Song Dynasty and is still observed.

2. Miaozitou: name of a place.

3. Liuhe Tower: a famous wooden tower by the Qiantang River.

七十四　弄潮 [1]

　　吳兒善泅者數百，皆披髮文身。手持十幅大彩旗，爭先鼓勇，溯迎而上，出沒于鯨波萬仞中，騰身百變，而旗尾略不沾濕，以此夸能。而豪民貴宦，爭賞銀彩。

宋　周密《武林舊事》

【語譯】

　　吳地幾百個擅長游泳的男子，都披散着頭髮紋了身。[他們] 手裏拿着十面大的彩旗，爭先恐後，鼓起勇氣，迎着 [波濤] 逆流而上，在萬丈高的驚濤駭浪中 [一會兒] 出現，[一會兒] 隱沒，[他們] 騰躍着，身體的動作千姿百態，變化無窮，但 [手中] 旗子的邊緣卻幾乎沒被水沾濕，[弄潮兒] 用這來炫耀 [自己的] 技能。而富豪權貴們爭先賞給 [他們] 銀錢和彩綢。

【註釋】

1. 弄潮：在波濤洶湧的水面上表演各種技能。流行於杭州等地區的民間娛樂活動。每年夏曆八月觀潮時進行。

74   Playing with the Tide[1]

Hair streaming free, bodies tattooed, hands clutching big colourful flags in sets of ten, hundreds of swimmers from the Wu area compete in breasting the tidal surge. Appearing and disappearing amidst the mountainous waves, they leap into kaleidoscopic patterns, holding their flags aloft without wetting even so much as their edges. Such are the displays of their competence and skill that the rich and powerful are eager to shower them with gifts of silver and silk.

Zhou Mi (Song Dynasty):
Past Events of the Martial Arts World

Notes:

1. Playing with the tide: to display one's swimming skill atop turbulent waves, an entertainment popular among common people in the areas around Hangzhou. It is undertaken in lunar August in the tide-watching season.

七十五　暖房 [1]

　　或有新搬移來居止之人，則鄰人爭借動事，遺獻湯茶，指引買賣之類，則見睦鄰之義，又率錢物，安排酒食，以為之賀，謂之"暖房"。

　　　　　　　　　　　　宋　吳自牧《夢粱錄》

【語譯】

　　[如果] 有 [從別處] 新搬遷來的人，那麼 [他的] 鄰居都爭先恐後地借 [給他] 日常應用的器具，送湯送茶 [給他喝]，並介紹商業經營等類的事，由此可見到 [他們] 與鄰居友愛和睦的情義。還有出錢出物，安排酒食，以祝賀 [新鄰居喬遷之喜]，這稱作"暖房"。

【註釋】

1. 暖房：民間認為，"遠親不如近鄰"。為遷入新居的鄰人送禮、祝賀，是流傳至今的一種習俗。

75 Housewarming[1]

When a newcomer moves in, people in the neighbourhood compete to lend him household utensils, send him soup
and tea and introduce him to commerce in the vicinity. This
demonstrates the friendly and harmonious relationship among
the neighbours. They also chip in money and things and throw
a party as a gesture of their best wishes for his new household.
This practice is called "housewarming".

Wu Zimu (Song Dynasty):
Records of a Pipe Dream

Notes:

1. Housewarming: Common people believe that "neighbours are
   dearer than distant relatives". To send gifts and congratulations to
   a newcomer is a custom that has been passed on to the present
   day.

七十六　僧人報曉

　　每日交四更，諸山寺觀已鳴鐘，庵舍行者頭陀[1]，打鐵板兒或木魚兒沿街報曉，各分地方。若晴則曰“天色晴明”……陰則曰“天色陰晦”，雨則言雨。……雖風雨霜雪，不敢缺此。每月朔望及遇節序，則沿門求乞齋糧[2]。

　　　　　　　　　　　宋　吳自牧《夢粱錄》

【語譯】

　　每天 [清晨] 剛剛到四更時，各山上的佛寺道觀已響起了 [晨] 鐘，住在草房中的苦行僧人就敲打着鐵板兒或木魚兒沿街報告 [人們] 天亮了，[他們] 各人有 [自己] 報時的地方。如果天晴，他們就叫喊“天氣晴朗”，天陰就報告“天色陰晦”，下雨時就說“下雨了”。即使遇到了颱風下雨降霜落雪的天氣，也不敢耽誤此事。夏曆每月的初一和十五以及遇到節日，[他們] 就逐家逐戶地去乞求施捨食物。

【註釋】

1. 行者頭陀：行腳乞食的苦行僧人。
2. 齋糧：僧人向人所乞求的飯食。

202

76   Monks Heralding Daybreak

At the fourth watch in the morning when the bells of the Buddhist temples and Taoist monasteries in the mountains chime, the ascetic monks in thatched huts start to beat either iron plates or *muyuer*[1] along the streets to herald the break of day, each patrolling his own section. If it is sunny, they shout, "The sun shines brightly!" If it is cloudy they announce, "It is cloudy and gloomy!" If it rains they report the rain. They never put off their rounds even in such extremes of weather as wind, rain, frost or snow. On the 1st and 15th of every lunar month and during festivals they beg for alms and food from door to door.

Wu Zimu (Song Dynasty):
Records of a Pipe Dream

Notes:

1. *muyuer*: i.e., "wooden fish", a percussion instrument made of a hollow wooden block, usually used by Buddhist priests to beat rhythm when chanting scriptures.

七十七　手影戲 [1]

[僧惠明] 嘗遇手影戲者，人請之占頌，即把筆書云：
三尺生綃作戲臺，全憑十指逞詼諧，有時明月燈窗下，一
笑還從掌握來。

宋　洪邁《夷堅志》

雜手藝皆有巧名……手影戲。……以手勢向燈取影，
作種種姿式為戲。

宋　耐得翁《都城紀勝》

【語譯】

[惠明和尚] 有次遇到演手影戲的藝人，人們請他即興作詩，
他立即提起筆寫道：三尺生絲作演戲的舞台，[內容] 有趣又引
人發笑全靠十個手指來表現。常常在明月夜點着燈的窗下[表演]，
[觀眾的] 笑聲是由 [他們的] 手中來的啊。

雜技手藝都有巧妙的名稱，[如] 手影戲，[這是] 用手的姿勢
依靠燈光得到影子，[演員] 作出各種各樣的手的姿態進行演出。

【註釋】

1. 手影戲：南宋時流行於江浙一帶的民間娛樂。表演者藉着燈光或月
   光，把手指演出的各種形像投影在面前的綢布上，生動有趣。

77   Hand-Shadow Drama[1]

Once Monk Huiming met some hand-shadow artists who requested him to compose a poem. Brush in his hand, he improvised:

Three feet of silk make up the stage.
Ten fingers entertain the audience.
By the candle-lit window on a moonlit night,
Laughter bursts out of the palms.

Hong Mai (Song Dynasty):
Records of Yijian

All kinds of hand art take clever names, such as the "hand-shadow play". The artists' simple hand movements in the lamplight cast a myriad of dramatic shadows.

Nai Deweng (Song Dynasty):
Records of Famous Events in the Capital

Notes:

1. Hand-shadow drama: a popular entertainment that prevailed in Jiangsu and Zhejiang provinces in the Southern Song Dynasty.

七十八　抽陀螺[1]

　　陀螺者，木製如小空鐘，中實而無柄，繞以鞭之繩而無竹尺。卓于地，急掣其鞭，一掣，陀螺則轉，無聲也，視其緩而鞭之，轉轉無復住。轉之疾，正如卓立地上，頂光旋旋，影不動也。

明　劉侗　于奕正《帝京景物略》

【語譯】

　　陀螺，用木頭製成，像小銅鐘[的樣子]，中間是實心的，沒有柄，把繩子繞在上面抽打它，繩上沒有小竹棍連着。[把它]直立在地上，急速地抽打，一抽打，陀螺就轉了，[轉的時候]沒有聲音。看它轉得慢起來了，[馬上再]抽打它，就又轉啊轉地不再停住了。轉得快[的時候]，就像直立在地上一樣，頂部的光在不停地旋轉，[但是它的]影子[絲紋]不動。

【註釋】

1. 抽陀螺：流傳至今的民間的兒童遊戲，通常在冬春季節進行。

78 Whipping a Top[1]

A top is a wooden toy in the shape of a little copper bell, except that it is solid and it has no handle. A [whip] string is wound around it, with no bamboo rod attached. Once the top is set on the ground, you must whip it speedily. When whipped, the top spins quickly and silently. As soon as it begins to slow down, you whip it again. Thus, it spins on and on. When it spins fast, it looks as if it were standing still on the ground. The glittering surface gyrates incessantly while its shadow remains still.

Liu Tong and Yu Yizheng (Ming Dynasty) :
Scenery and Events in the Capital

Notes:

1. Whipping a top: a popular children's game, usually played during winter and spring times.

七十九　踏歌 [1]

十月十五日……相與連臂踏地為節，歌《赤鳳凰來》。

晉　葛洪《西京雜記》

百錢可得酒斗 [2] 許，雖非社日 [3] 長聞鼓；吳 [4] 兒踏歌女起舞，但道快樂無所苦。

宋　王安石《後元豐行》

【語譯】

十月十五日，[女人] 相互挽着手臂用腳踏地作為節拍，唱着《赤鳳凰來》這首歌。

一百錢可喝到一斗多的酒，即使不是祭祀土地神的日子也常 [能] 聽到鼓聲；吳地的男人腳踏地為節拍唱着歌，女人跳起了舞，[這可真是] 只有快樂而沒有苦惱啊。

208

79   Stomping Songs[1]

On the fifteenth day of the tenth lunar month women sing the song, "Here Comes the Red Phoenix", stomping the ground arm in arm rhythmically.

Ge Hong (Jin Dynasty):
Miscellanies of the West Capital

Drinking ten litres plus of wine for only a hundred copper coins,
    Hearing the drumbeats though it is not earth god's day[2],
    In the Wu[3] area, men sing as their feet stomp out the rhythm and women dance:
    Such are the days filled with happiness and no sorrow.

Wang Anshi (Song Dynasty):
After the Journey to Yuanfeng

【註釋】

1. 踏歌：唱歌時腳踏地作節拍，並伴有舞蹈動作。這是古代的一種民間歌舞形式。

2. 斗：古代的酒器。

3. 社日：古代祭祀土地神的日子。這天男女都要停止工作，女人甚至連針綫活也不做。

4. 吳：古國名。指今天的江蘇、上海的大部分和安徽、浙江的一部分地區。

Notes:

1. Stomping songs: i.e., stamping out the rhythm of the song while singing, accompanied by dance gestures. This was a form of folk song and dance in ancient times.

2. earth god's day: the day when people offered sacrifices to the earth god in ancient times. On this day all work was forbidden, even women's sewing.

3. Wu: the name of an ancient state. It covered the major parts of Jiangsu and Shanghai and parts of Anhui and Zhejiang.

八十　踩高蹺[1]

　　踩高蹺，雙木續足之戲。按此戲之起頗古。《列子》：“宋有蘭子以技干宋元君，以雙枝高倍其身，屬其脛，并驅并馳。”

李鑒堂《俗語考源》

　　置丈許木于足下，可以超乘，謂之踏高喬。

清　顧祿《清嘉錄》

【語譯】

　　踩高蹺，是用兩根木頭接上雙腳的表演。追究起來這種表演的起源甚為古老。《列子》[這本書中說道]：“宋國有個叫蘭子的人，用他的技藝取悅宋元君。將兩根高過自己身體一倍的木棍連接他的小腿部分，又能行走，又能疾走。”

　　把一丈餘長的木頭安放在腳下，[木頭]能載着[他]前進，稱作“踏高喬”。

【註釋】

1. 踩高蹺：也稱“踏高喬”、“扎高腳”。表演者腳繫高高的木製長棍，化妝成各種傳說故事中的人物表演動作。此傳統民間的表演活動，通常在節日中進行，至今仍常見。

80 Walking on Stilts[1]

Walking on stilts is a performance which employs two lengths of wood strapped to the feet. This kind of performance can be traced back to very ancient origins. It is described in Liezi, "There was a man named Lanzi in the State of Song (circa 7th century B.C.) who entertained the first Song emperor with his feat of walking and running with two wooden poles taller than himself attached to his lower legs".

Li Jiantang: The Etymology of Idioms

Attaching wooden sticks over three metres long to one's feet and walking on them is called "walking on stilts".

Gu Lu (Qing Dynasty):
Worthy Records of the Qing Dynasty

Notes:

1. Walking on stilts: also termed "tied-on long feet". Performers are dressed as lengendary characters and perform with long poles attached to their feet. It is a holiday folk performance.

213

八十一　傀儡戲 [1]

　　圍布作房，支以一木，五指運三寸傀儡，金鼓喧闐，詞白則用叫頹子，均一人為之，俗呼木頭人戲。牽絲戲，彷彿傀儡，手足皆以絲牽運動，故名。

清　顧祿《清嘉錄》

【語譯】

　　把布圍成一個棚子，用一根木頭支撐着，五個手指操縱着三寸〔大小〕的木頭人。鑼鼓喧天，〔戲中的人物〕是拿故意壓尖了的嗓音來對白的，〔一切〕全是由一個人擔任的，民間稱這為木頭人戲。牽絲戲，和木頭人戲差不多，只是〔木偶的〕手和腳都用絲綫牽連着活動，所以叫作〔牽絲戲這個〕名字。

【註釋】

1. 傀儡戲：用木偶來表演故事的戲劇。通常演員在幕後一邊操縱木偶，一邊說旁白及演唱。因木偶的形體和操縱技術不同，有布袋木偶、提綫木偶、杖頭木偶等類的區別。此傳統民間表演藝術至今仍廣為流行。

81 Puppet Drama[1]

A piece of cloth is framed into an open-sided box supported on a pole. The puppets, several inches tall, are manipulated on the performer's hands accompanied by gong and drum. The dialogue is spoken shrilly by a single narrator. This kind of drama is locally called "wooden people play". A similar version, the "string-drawn play", takes its name because the hands and feet of the puppets are suspended on pieces of string.

Gu Lu (Qing Dynasty):
Worthy Records of the Qing Dynasty

Notes:

1. Puppet drama: a kind of drama in which the play is performed by puppets. The puppeteers stand behind the stage manipulating the puppet as well as singing and reciting the lines. Differentiated by the forms of the puppets and the methods of manipulation, the puppet drama is divided into categories of "sack puppet (or glove puppet)", "string puppet" and "rod puppet". This form of folk art is still performed today.

八十二　猴戲[1]

　　鳳陽人蓄猴，令其自為冠帶，并豢犬為猴之乘，能為
《磨坊》、《三戰》諸齣，俗呼猢猻撮把戲。

　　　　　　　　　　　　　　　　清　顧祿《清嘉錄》

【語譯】

　　安徽鳳陽人馴養了猴子，叫它自己戴帽子繫腰帶，還餵養了
狗作為猴子的乘騎。[它們] 能表演《磨坊》、《三戰》等各齣戲，民
間稱作猢猻耍把戲。

【註釋】

1. 猴戲：民間藝人馴化的猴子流動演出的戲。通常在一空地上先由藝人
　　用鑼鼓吸引觀眾，然後給猴子穿上紅衣，讓它戴上舊時的官帽等進行
　　各種表演。

82 Monkey Drama[1]

In Fengyang people train monkeys to dress themselves in hats and belts. These people raise dogs to be their monkeys' steeds. The monkeys are even able to stage such plays as "The Mill", "Three Battles", etc. Local people call this kind of drama "monkey play".

Gu Lu (Qing Dynasty) :
Worthy Records of the Qing Dynasty

Notes:

1. Monkey drama: a play performed by monkeys tamed by folk artists. At the beginning of the play, folk artists beat gongs and drums to attract an audience. They then make the monkeys dress themselves up in the red clothes and hats of old-time government officials and do all kinds of tricks.

八十三　名帖¹交際

　　有遣僕投紅單刺²至戚若友家者，多不親往，答拜者亦如之，謂之飛帖。案：……褚人獲《堅瓠集》云："拜年帖，國初用古簡，有稱呼。康熙中，則易紅單，書某人拜賀。素無往還，道路不揖者，單亦及之。"

清　顧祿《清嘉錄》

　　長安有平康坊³，……京都俠少，萃集于此。兼每年新進士⁴以紅箋名紙，游謁其中。

五代　王仁裕《開元天寶遺事》

【語譯】

　　如有派遣僕人投送紅紙名帖去親戚朋友家[拜年]的人，大多數不再親自去[拜年]了。回拜的人也是這樣[用紅紙名帖答謝]，這[種做法]，稱作飛帖。按語：褚人獲在《堅瓠集》這本書說："拜年的名帖，清朝建國初，用古代信簡[的形式]，上有[受帖人的]稱呼。康熙時代中期改用紅色的紙，[上面]寫着某某人拜賀。[有些]一向沒有往來的人，在路上相見都不[相互]作揖問候的人，[拜年的]紅帖也[照樣]送給他。

83 Socializing by Means of Calling Cards[1]

If a person sends a servant to deliver his red calling card to relatives or friends in the New Year, he usually does not pay a visit in person. The recipient may respond in the same way by returning his red calling card. This practice is called "winging cards". Zhu Renhuo's Collection of Hard Gourds comments on this custom as follows: "Greeting cards were sent as early as the beginning of the Qing Dynasty in the form of traditional letters with the addressee's name. During the middle of Emperor Kangxi's reign, red paper was used and a complimentary close became customary. Now such cards are exchanged between people who do not visit one another or even speak when they meet in the street."

Gu Lu (Qing Dynasty):
Worthy Records of the Qing Dynasty

Chivalrous young people like to gather in Pingkangfang[2] in Chang'an. At the same time, the new *jingshi*[3], flaunting their red name cards, make friends there.

Wang Renyu (Five Dynasties):
Incidents in the Years of Kai Yuan and Tian Bao

長安有個叫平康坊的地方，京城中見義勇為的年輕人，都匯聚在這兒。同時每年的新進士也用紅紙名帖在這裏交遊拜訪[各種人]。

【註釋】

1. 名帖：用紅紙書寫姓名、職銜，古代拜訪別人和與人聯繫時用的紙片。又稱"謁"、"名刺"、"名紙"，今稱"名片"。此交際習俗起源很早，原先是削木而成，後有了紙，才以紙代木做成"名帖"、"名紙"。

2. 紅單刺：指紅紙名帖。刺，是漢代時對名帖的稱呼。

3. 平康坊：唐代首都長安城中的地名，當時的妓女聚居之處。

4. 進士：指古代考取科舉最高一級考試的人。

Notes:

1. calling cards: a card in red paper with the name and title of the person used in communication and correspondence. It was given many names in ancient times. A modern version is the name card or business card. This social custom originated long ago. Originally, the card was made of wood. Later, with the invention of paper, it was called "name paper".

2. Pingkangfang: a place in Chang'an, capital of the Tang Dynasty. Courtesans thrived there then.

3. *jingshi*: a successful candidate in the highest imperial examinations.

八十四　唱喏禮[1]

古所謂揖[2]，但舉手而已。今所謂喏，乃始于江左[3]諸王。方其時，惟王氏子弟為之。故支道林入東見王子猷兄弟還，人問：“諸王何如？”答曰：“見一羣白項鳥，但聞喚啞啞聲。”今之喏也。

宋　陸游《老學庵筆記》

【語譯】

古代所說的作揖，只是舉起手而已。現在所說的唱喏，[即作揖同時出聲致敬]，是從東面姓王的各個人開始的。在那個時候，只有王家的人這樣做。所以支道林去東面見到王子猷兄弟後回來，有人問他：“王氏各位怎麼樣？”支道林回答說：“看見一羣白頸項的鳥，只能聽見[他們]啞啞的叫喚聲。”這，就是現在[所說]的唱喏。

【註釋】

1. 唱喏禮：古代男子所行的一種禮節，舉起雙手放在胸前作拱手禮時，嘴中同時發出聲音。
2. 揖：作揖，古代的拱手禮。
3. 江左：指長江下游以東地區。

84 Saluting by *Re*[1]

In ancient times one saluted by yi[2], only raising one's hands. Our modern *re* salute originated with a family named Wang who lived in the lower reaches of the Yangtze River. This special method of greeting was practised first by the Wang brothers. When Zhi Daolin returned from the east where he had visited the Wang Ziyou brothers, he was asked, "How are the Wangs?" He replied, "What I saw was a flock of white-necked cranes cawing at each other." This greeting is what we call *re* today.

Lu You (Song Dyansty):
Notes Written in Lao Xue Study

Notes:

1. Saluting by *re*: a mode of salutation between men in ancient times. In addition to raising their hands clasped in front of their chests, they also uttered a greeting sound.

2. *yi*: or *zuo yi*, an ancient way of saluting people by bowing and raising both hands which are clasped at the same time.

八十五 雀竿之戲 [1]

是日，觀 [2] 中有雀竿之戲，其法，樹長竿于庭，高可三丈，一人攀緣而上，舞蹈其顛，盤旋上下，……變態多方。觀者目瞪神驚汗流浹背，而為此技者，如蝶拍鴉翻，蓬蓬然自若也。

明　田汝成《西湖游覽志餘》

【語譯】

[夏曆三月三日] 這天，道觀裏有 [名叫] 雀竿的 [雜技] 表演。這種表演辦法是，在庭院中豎上一根 [粗粗的] 長竹竿，三丈多高，一個人沿着竹竿 [從下] 向上攀登，在竹竿的頂部舞蹈，上上下下盤旋，[動作] 千姿百態，變化多端。觀眾看得目瞪口呆，神情緊張，以至汗流浹背，而表演者卻如蝴蝶展翅，鴉雀翻身，[一副] 悠然自得，輕鬆如常的 [樣子]。

【註釋】

1. 雀竿之戲：一種傳統的雜技節目，由經過訓練的民間藝人演出，至今仍可見到。

2. 觀：道觀。傳說夏曆三月三日是道教北極佑聖真君的生日，所以此日觀中有各種慶祝儀式和表演活動。

85 "Sparrow on a Bamboo Tip"[1]

On the third day of the third lunar month[2], performers put on acrobatic shows called "Sparrow on a Bamboo Tip" in Taoist temples. First, a bamboo pole over ten metres tall is erected in a courtyard. Then the performers climb to its top and dance there. They slide up and down and strike manifold poses. The audience are agape. So tensely are they watching that they drip with sweat. On the other hand, the performers are as carefree and leisurely as butterflies fluttering their wings or crows swooping.

Tian Rucheng (Ming Dynasty):
Notes on West Lake Tour

Notes:

1. "Sparrow on a Bamboo Tip": a traditional show put on by trained folk artistes. Similar versions are still performed.

2. the third day of the third lunar month: It is believed that that day is the birthday of an important Taoist saint, Beiji Yousheng Zhenjun. Hence, there are various celebrations and performances on that day in Taoist temples.

八十六　盲人賣唱[1]

　　男女瞽者，多學琵琶，唱古今小説，平話，以覓衣食，謂之陶真。大抵説宋時事，蓋汴京[2]遺俗也。瞿宗吉過汴梁詩云：“歌舞樓臺事可夸。昔年曾此擅奢華，……陌頭盲女無愁恨，能撥琵琶説趙家[3]。”其俗殆與杭無異。

　　　　　　　　　　明　田汝成《西湖游覽志餘》

【語譯】

　　男女盲人大多都學習琵琶，唱古代和當今的傳説軼聞和故事，用此換取温飽，這稱為“陶真”。[他們]大致都是敍説宋代的事情，這是[北宋]首都汴梁遺留的習俗。瞿宗吉的《過汴梁》詩中説：“廣廈大屋歌舞昇平的事值得誇耀，往昔這兒曾經恣意奢侈豪華。路邊的盲女無愁也無恨，[平靜地]撥弄着琵琶講述趙氏家族[的故事]”。[詩中所説的]這習俗與杭州的習俗沒有甚麼兩樣。

86 Blind People Singing for a Living[1]

To make a living, many blind people learn to play the *pipa*, and sing ballads or songs recounting traditional and contemporary events. This practice is called *taozhen* (truth singing). These songs are mainly about events in the Song Dynasty. This old custom has been passed down from the capital of the Northern Song Dynasty. In his poem, <u>Passing through Bianliang</u>, Qu Zongji wrote:

> It's worthwhile to boast of songs and dances in mansions
> Where a luxurious life was led in the olden times.
> By the roadside, carefree and sorrowless blind girls
> Retell stories of the Zhaos[2] while they pluck the *pipa*.

What is depicted in this poem is identical to the practice in Hangzhou.

Tian Rucheng (Ming Dynasty):
<u>Notes on West Lake Tour</u>

1. 盲人賣唱：盲人手持簡單的樂器，如胡琴、琵琶等沿街賣唱，靠路人所施捨的微薄錢財生活，此種習俗至今還偶然可見。

2. 汴京：指北宋的首都汴梁，今河南省開封市。

3. 趙家：宋代皇帝姓趙，故稱趙家，用以指宋代皇族。

Notes:

1. Blind people singing for a living: Blind people play simple musical instruments such as *huqing*, a two-stringed bow instrument, and *pipa*, a plucked string instrument with a fretted fingerboard, and sing along the streets to seek a living on the alms from the passers-by. This custom can occasionally be seen nowadays.

2. the Zhaos: The family name of the emperor of the Song Dynasty is Zhao. Thus, "the Zhaos" refers to the royal family.

八十七　行善[1]

　　有好善積德者,多是恤孤念苦,敬老憐貧。……或死無周身之具者,……則給散棺木,助其火葬,以終其事。或遇大雪,……凍餓于道者,富家沿門親察其孤苦艱難,遇夜以碎金銀或錢會插于門縫,以周其苦,俾侵晨展戶得之,如至天降。

宋　吳自牧《夢粱錄》

【語譯】

　　喜好行善積德的人,大多都體恤孤兒和關心受苦的人,尊敬老人憐憫窮人。有的人死了但沒有遮蔽身體的東西,[行善的人]就出錢給他買棺木,[或]幫助火葬,了結此人的後事。倘遇到了大雪天,路邊有挨凍受餓的人,[行善的]有錢人就逐家逐戶地親自察看他們艱難困苦的[情形],到了夜裏把小塊的金子銀子或紙錢插在[這些人家的]門縫中,用以周濟苦難。待到清晨他們開門得到這些錢,就像從天上落下來的一般。

【註釋】

1. 行善:民間篤信做善事積德,下一世會有好的報應,因而行善者不僅局限於富人。普通人行善即根據自己的能力和條件盡可能地為別人或為公眾做好事。

87 Doing Good Works[1]

People who like to do good works and strive for moral perfection tend to show concern for orphans, to care for the afflicted, to respect the aged and sympathize with the poor. If someone dies with nothing to cover his body, these philanthropists will donate money for his coffin or cremation. If people by the roadside suffer from cold and hunger in heavy snows, these rich people will visit their homes one by one to find out their difficulties. Then, to alleviate their misery, under cover of the night these philanthropists insert banknotes or gold and silver coins in the cracks of their doors. When the poor open their doors in the morning, this money rains down as if it had fallen from heaven.

Wu Zimu (Song Dynasty):
Records of a Pipe Dream

Notes:

1. Doing good works: Folk people believe that if you do good works and achieve moral perfection, you will be rewarded in your next incarnation. So philanthropists are found not only among the rich, ordinary people, too, as their status and fortune permit, also find opportunities to do good deeds.

八十八　貼花子[1]

今婦人面飾用花子，起自昭容上官氏所製，以掩點迹。大曆以前士大夫妻多妬悍者，婢妾小不如意，輒印面，故有月點、錢點。

唐　段成式《酉陽雜俎》

【語譯】

現在婦女用以裝飾面部的花子，開始是由女官上官氏所創造的，用來掩蓋臉上的斑點缺陷。唐代宗大曆年以前，官僚以及有社會地位的讀書人的妻子大多數是心懷嫉妬又十分兇惡 [的女人]，[家中的] 婢女、[丈夫的] 小妾稍有一點兒 [使她] 不滿意，就印 [傷她們的] 臉，所以有月斑、錢斑 [這樣的說法]。

【註釋】

1. 貼花子：也稱"貼花黃"。古代婦女喜用的一種面飾。用極薄的金屬片或黃紙作成星、月、花、葉或蟲鳥形，貼於額部、臉部，以示美觀。也常用來掩蓋臉部斑點。

88　Wearing Beauty Spots[1]

Modern women's "flowerpieces", the beauty spots worn to cover freckles and facial blemishes, were created by Shang Guan Shi, a supervisor of palace women in the Tang Dynasty. Before the year of Dali (766-780), the wives of government officials and high-status scholars were a vicious and jealous lot. At the slightest provocation, they scarred the faces of maids or concubines with marks which were so common that various types had names such as "coin spot" or "crescent moon spot".

Duan Chengshi (Tang Dynasty) :
You Yang Records of a Myriad Things

Notes:

1. Wearing beauty spots: also called "wearing flower yellow", was a kind of facial decoration for women in ancient times. The "flowers" were made of very thin metal pieces or yellow paper in the shapes of stars, moons, flowers, leaves, birds or insects to be glued on the forehead or face as an adornment. They were also worn to cover up facial blemishes.

八十九　戴柏子花

年夜，像生花舖[1]以柏葉點銅綠，并翦彩絨為虎形，紮成小朵，曰老虎花。……或翦人物為壽星[2]、和合[3]、招財進寶[4]、麒麟送子[5]之類，多取吉讖，號為柏子花。閨閣[6]中買以相饋貽，并為新年小兒女助裝。

清　顧祿《清嘉錄》

【語譯】

大年夜時，像生花店將柏樹葉子染了銅綠色，用彩色的絨剪成老虎的形狀，紮在一起成小朵，名叫老虎花。有的剪出壽星、和合二仙、招財進寶、麒麟送子之類的人物 [形狀]，大多數是 [為了] 取吉利的兆頭，稱之為柏子花。婦女們買來相互贈送，並且在新年的時候用它來打扮小男孩和小女孩。

【註釋】

1. 像生花舖：仿製天然花果和製作人物等的工藝品商店。
2. 壽星：民間信仰中的長壽之神。
3. 和合：民間傳說中象徵吉祥如意的神。原為一神，後衍化成二神，稱"和合二仙"。
4. 招財進寶：民間信仰中掌管錢財之神的形像。
5. 麒麟送子：民間認為求拜麒麟可生育得子，故麒麟上騎一小孩的形像為吉祥的象徵。
6. 閨閣：婦女的臥室。常用以指古代婦女。

89 Wearing Cypress Flowers

Artificial flower shops have a New Year's Eve specialty: a bouquet made by dyeing cypress leaves copper green and ornamenting them with tiger images cut from colourful knitting wool. These leaves are called tiger flowers. In addition to tigers, other images are used: the "longevity star", the "god of harmony", the "god of wealth", and the *qilin*[1] — all intended to elicit fortunate outcomes. Women send these cypress flower corsages to one another, and they dress up children with these ornaments in the New Year.

Gu Lu (Qing Dynasty):
Worthy Records of the Qing Dynasty

Notes:

1. *qilin*: a legendary animal the shape of which is similar to a deer with horns, scales and a long tail. In ancient times it was a propitious symbol. Common people believed that if you worshipped it and offered prayers to it you would inevitably have a son. So the *qilin* image was always associated with a small boy.

九十　染指甲[1]

鳳仙花紅者，用葉搗碎，入明礬少許，在內先洗淨指甲，然後以此敷甲上，用片帛纏定過夜，初染色淡連，染三五次，其色若胭脂，洗滌不去，可經旬至退甲方漸去之。

宋　弁陽　周密《癸辛雜識》

鳳草飛紅，繡女敲而染指。

清　潘榮陛《帝京歲時紀勝》

【語譯】

[選] 紅色的鳳仙花，用葉子把它搗碎，加入一點兒明礬。先在內室中將手指甲洗乾淨，然後把這 [混合物] 敷在指甲上，用小片的綢子纏住固定一夜。第一次染的時候，顏色淡淡的，染了三五次以後，指甲的顏色就像胭脂 [那樣紅]，洗都洗不掉，可長達十天到剪指甲時才漸漸地褪去。

鳳仙花紅了，繡花女 [把它的汁] 搾 [出來] 染手指甲。

【註釋】

1. 染指甲：用鳳仙花汁染指甲，是民間婦女的妝飾習俗，流行於很多地區。

236

90 Dyeing Fingernails

Select red garden balsam petals, pound them in a mortar and add a pinch of alum. Cleanse your fingernails in your chamber and apply the mixture to them. Bind them with a piece of silk and let the mixture set overnight. At the first application the colour is pale, but after three to five treatments it will be dark as rouge and will not wash away. It will fade by the time the fingernails are trimmed in ten days.

Bian Yang and Zhou Mi (Song Dynasty):
Miscellanies in the Year of Guixin

When the garden balsams turn red, embroidery girls extract the juice to dye their fingernails.

Pan Rongbi (Qing Dynasty):
Famous Events in the Capital

九十一　點燕脂[1]

《古今注》曰，燕草出西方，葉似薊，花似茜，土人以染粉，為婦人面色，故名燕脂。……秦宮中悉紅妝，當是其物自秦始也。

宋　高承《事物紀原》

南都石黛[2]，最發雙蛾[3]，北地燕脂，偏開兩靨[4]。

南朝陳　徐陵《玉臺新咏序》

【語譯】

《古今注》[這本書]說，燕草是西方 [燕國] 出產的，葉子像薊草，花的形狀如茜草花一般，當地人用 [它的汁] 染了粉，作為婦女臉上 [紅色] 的化妝物，所以名叫燕脂。秦代皇宮中 [的女人]全是用紅色作為面飾的，因此 [燕脂] 應當是從秦代起源的。

南方都城的青黑色的顏料，最能使美女的雙眉動人，北方的燕脂，展開了 [美女] 兩頰 [微笑的] 酒窩。

91 Putting on Rouge

According to the <u>Annotations of Ancient and Modern Times</u>, *yan* grass grew in the western state of Yan[1]. Its leaves were like the setose thistle, its flowers were like the madder. Local people dyed powder with its juice to make rouge, a facial cosmetic. Palace women in the Qin Dynasty all put on such rouge. This probably indicates that rouge originated in the Qin Dynasty.

Gao Cheng (Song Dynasty):
<u>The Origins of Things</u>

The kohl[2] of the southern metropolises is best for decorating the eyebrows, while the rouge of the north makes dimples blossom.

Xu Ling (Southern Dynasties, the State of Chen):
<u>Preface to New Ode to Yutai</u>

【註釋】

1. 點燕脂：婦女用一種紅色的化妝物塗在臉頰或嘴唇上。此習俗起源甚早。

2. 石黛：一種青黑色的顏料。

3. 雙蛾：指美女的兩眉。

4. 靨：酒窩。

Notes:

1. Yan: one of the ancient states in China during the Spring and Autumn Period (770 B.C. - 476 B.C.) and the Warring States Period (475 B.C. - 221 B.C.).

2. kohl: a preparation used by women in the East to darken the edges of their eyebrows.

九十二　百事大吉[1]

簽柏枝于柿餅[2]，以大桔承之，謂之百事大吉。

明　田汝成《西湖游覽志餘》

正月朔日元旦，食乾柿和桔子，曰"百事大吉"。

清　光緒《武進陽湖縣志》

【語譯】

把柏枝插在柿餅上，下面墊着大桔子，稱作"百事大吉"。

[夏曆] 正月初一元旦這天，[人們] 吃乾柿子和桔子，説是"百事大吉"。

【註釋】

1. 百事大吉：民間節日祈吉食品。因柏樹諧音"百"，柿子諧音"事"，桔子與"吉利"的"吉"諧音，故稱"百事大吉"。此習俗流行於江浙地區。

2. 柿餅：即乾柿子，整個柿子晾乾後，成扁圓形狀，故稱"柿餅"。

242

92 "All is Well"[1]

Cypress twigs are inserted into dried persimmons atop big tangerines. This arrangement is called "all is well".

Tian Rucheng (Ming Dynasty):
Notes on West Lake Tour

On Lunar New Year's Day, people eat dried persimmons and tangerines. This practice is called "all is well".

(Year of Guangxu, Qing Dynasty):
Annual Record of Yanghu County, Wujin

Notes:

1. "All is well": Dried persimmons and tangerines are regarded as auspicious food among commoners. This is because the pronunciation of "persimmon" and "tangerine" in Chinese are homonymous with the words "thing" and "auspicious" respectively. Therefore, when put together, these two fruits suggest that "all things are auspicious", i.e. "all is well". This eating habit is popular in Jiangsu and Zhejiang provinces.

九十三　吃齋[1]

世人以茹素為齋戒，豈知聖賢之所謂齋者，齊也，齊其心之所不齊，所謂戒者，齋戒其非心妄念也。

明　陶宗儀《説郛》引李之彥《東谷所見》

【語譯】

世上的人把吃素稱為齋戒，殊不知聖人賢者所認為的"齋"，是齊的意思，即把那心中雜亂[的東西]理齊；[他們]所認為的"戒"，是戒除那些不該[存在]心中的非份念頭。

【註釋】

1.　吃齋：即吃素食，也稱茹素、素食、吃素等。漢族中信仰佛教者的飲食習俗，流傳至今約有千年以上歷史。分吃長齋和吃花齋兩種。吃長齋的人終年食素，吃花齋的人只在特定的日子裏食素。吃齋時，不食任何動物的肉、油和蛋。

93 Practising Abstinence[1]

Common people practise vegetarianism as a form of fasting and abstinence. But they do not know that according to saints and sages, so-called fasting is to put in order disorderly thinking, and so-called abstinence is to quell inordinate desires.

Tao Zongyi (Ming Dynasty):
Talking about Outer Town
quoting Li Zhiyan's
Experience in the East Valley

Notes:

1. Practising abstinence: popularly called "eating only vegetables", a diet custom observed by Buddhists of the Han race for over a thousand years. It is classified into two categories: "long abstinence" when people eat vegetables all year long, and "flower abstinence" when people eat vegetables only on certain special days. When practising abstinence, people avoid meat, eggs, and animal oils.

九十四　臘八粥[1]

　　八日，則寺院[2]及人家用胡桃、松子、乳蕈、柿、栗之類為粥，謂之“臘八粥”。

宋　周密《武林舊事》

　　臘八粥者，用黃米、白米、江米、小米、菱角米、栗子、紅江豆、去皮棗泥等，合水煮熟，外用染紅桃仁、杏仁、瓜子、花生、榛穰、松子及白糖、紅糖、瑣瑣葡萄，以作點染。

清　富察敦崇《燕京歲時記》

【語譯】

　　[臘月]八日，佛寺和普通老百姓家用胡桃、松子、小傘菌、柿餅和栗子之類[的乾果糧食]做成粥，叫做“臘八粥”。

　　臘八粥，是用黃米、白米、糯米、小米、菱角米、栗子、紅豇豆和去皮的棗泥等放上水煮熟，最上面用染成紅色的桃仁、杏仁、瓜子、花生、榛子仁、松子仁以及白糖、紅糖和細碎的葡萄乾點綴。

246

94   Rice Porridge for December Eighth[1]

On the eighth day of the twelfth lunar month, temples[2] and households cook porridge with walnuts, pine seeds, small mushrooms, persimmons, chestnuts and so forth. The porridge is called "rice porridge for December Eighth".

Zhou Mi (Song Dynasty) :
Past Events of the Martial Arts World

To cook "rice porridge for December Eighth", boil yellow rice, white rice, glutinous rice, millet, chestnuts, red cowpeas and jujube paste together. When it is done, dot it with walnuts, apricot kernels, melon seeds, peanuts, hazelnuts, pine nuts, all dyed red, and white sugar, brown sugar and chopped raisins.

Fucha Duncong (Qing Dynasty)
Annual Records of the Capital

【註釋】

1. 臘八粥：臘月（即夏曆十二月）八日是古代歲末祭祀百神的日子，這天民間普遍吃粥，故稱為"臘八粥"，今俗稱"八寶粥"。其來源有多種。

2. 寺院：臘八粥的來源之一起於佛教。傳說佛教創始人釋迦牟尼，曾在飢餓中吃了一頓加了野果的粥，於是得道成佛。這一天正夏曆是臘月初八。此後每年這天佛寺都要誦經唸法，煮臘八粥，以示紀念。

Notes:

1. Rice Porridge for December Eighth: The 8th of lunar December is the day when people offer sacrifices to all the gods. It is customary to eat rice porridge with nuts and dried fruits on that day. This dish is also called "rice porridge of eight treasures". There are many versions of the origins of this custom.

2. temples: One origin of this custom comes from Buddhism. Legends have it that once, famished, the founder of Buddhism, Sakyamuni, ate porridge cooked with wild fruits and was enlightened and became the Buddha. That happened on the eighth of lunar December. Therefore, on that day every year, monks in temples chant sutras and cook rice porridge with nuts and dried fruits to commemorate this event.

九十五　天井[1]

　　今江以南，人多稱庭墀際曰天井。……以其四周檐宇高而此獨下也。愚據周禮測之，似以其上露天，下設井，因謂之天井。井者，漏井，屋舍前受水潦之所。

清　翟灝《通俗編》

【語譯】

　　現今長江以南的人們大多將庭院至台階 [這塊地方] 稱作天井，因為四周的屋檐很高，而唯獨井的位置在下方。我根據《周禮》推測，似乎是因為上面露着天空，下面設置着井，因而稱作天井。井，就是漏井，屋子前面受到雨水沖擊的地方。

【註釋】

1.　天井：指房子與房子或房子與圍牆所圍成的露天空地，人們常種花養魚用以點綴。全國大部分地區的民居至今仍保持着天井。

95 "Sky Well"[1]

People south of the Yangtze River call their courtyard their "sky well" because, surrounded by buildings with high roofs, this opening lies low like a well in the ground. According to Zhou's Book of Rites, we can infer that this area is called a "sky well" because it is open to the sky above, and at ground level is a sunken area fed by rainwater.

Zhai Hao (Qing Dynasty):
Articles on Popular Things

Notes:

1. "Sky well": refers to an open area encircled by houses or walls. People usually plant flowers or rear fish to beautify it. This practice is popular in most parts of China.

九十六　鴟吻[1]

　　柏梁殿災，後越[2]巫言，海中有魚，虬尾似鴟，激浪即降雨，遂作其像于屋，以厭火祥。

　　　　　　宋　李誡《營造法式》卷二引《漢紀》

【語譯】

　　[漢代] 柏梁殿遭到了火災。此後，越地的巫師說，海中有 [一種] 魚，龍尾巴的形狀似鴟鷹，[牠的尾部] 一拍擊海浪立即就下雨了。於是 [人們] 在宮殿房屋 [的屋脊兩端] 作牠的像，作為避免火災的祥物。

【註釋】

1. 鴟吻：也叫"鴟尾"。傳統建築屋脊兩端的一種飾物。起初形如一名為蚩的海獸的尾部，後式樣改變，折而向上似張口吞脊，故稱鴟吻。流行於全國各地，至今仍隨處可見。
2. 越：古國名。疆域包括今江蘇、安徽、江西、浙江幾省的部份地區。

96 "Sparrow Hawk's Kiss"[1]

After Boliang Palace was burned in the Han Dynasty,
warlocks from the ancient state of Yue spoke of a legendary
sea fish. This creature has a tail shaped like a sparrow hawk's
which slaps against the waves and precipitates downpours.
So, people carve figures of this fish and place them at both
ends of the ridgepoles of buildings as a fire prevention charm.

Li Jie (Song Dynasty):
Architectural Designs, Book II,
quoting Records of Han Dynasty

Notes:

1. "sparrow hawk's kiss": also named "sparrow hawk's tail", a
   decorative figure on the two ends of a ridgepole. Originally in
   the shape of the tail of a sea beast called *chi*, the form evolved
   into a backward-curving bird, opening its beak as if to swallow
   the ridgepole — hence its name, "sparrow hawk's kiss". This
   architectural ornament can be seen anywhere in China.

九十七　店幌

　　不用字，不繪形，直揭其物于門外，或以象形之物代之，因其人多不識字也。如賣酒者懸酒一壺，賣炭者懸炭一支，而麵店則懸紙條，魚店則懸木魚，俗所謂幌子[1]者是也。

徐珂《清稗類鈔》

【語譯】

　　商店不寫字，[也] 不畫圖形，直接在門外亮出它 [所賣的] 東西，或者用與它形狀相像的東西代替。因人們多不識字之故。例如，賣酒的商店就懸一壺酒，賣炭的商店高掛一支炭；而麵店 [外]掛的是紙條，魚店懸著的是一條木頭造的魚。民間所說的幌子就是這些 [東西]。

【註釋】

1. 幌子：也稱"望子"。商店門外表明所賣的物品的標誌。此商業習俗流傳至今。

97 Shop Signs

Some shops exhibited neither painted signs nor written names. Instead, the owners displayed their goods, or dummy versions or symbols of them at their store fronts as they were illiterate. For instance, winesellers hung up a winepot, charcoal burners a piece of charcoal; noodle shops made do with strips of paper, and fish stalls displayed wooden fish. These are what common people called "shop signs".

Xu Ke : Classified Anecdotes of the Qing Dynasty

九十八 吟叫 [1]

　　京師凡賣一物，必有聲韻，其吟哦俱不同，故市人採其聲調，間以辭章，以為戲樂也。今盛于世，又謂之吟叫也。

宋　高承《事物紀原》

　　今街市和宅院，往往效京師叫聲，以市井諸色歌叫賣物之聲，採和宮商 [2] 成其詞也。

宋　吳自牧《夢粱錄》

【語譯】

　　京城中凡是賣一樣東西，都必定有 [它固定] 韻律的叫賣聲，它們吟叫聲全都不同，所以市民採用它們的韻調，配上唱詞，以此作成樂曲，現在非常盛行。這又稱為吟叫。

　　現今街上或 [人們的] 家裏，常常在模仿首都 [買賣人] 的叫賣聲，就是用市場上各色各樣的叫賣商品的聲韻，配上音樂作成詞曲的。

【註釋】

1. 吟叫：也稱"市聲"。市場上商人含有韻律的叫賣和吆喝稱吟叫，這種習俗流傳至今。
2. 宮商：指音樂。

98   Crying One's Wares

The distinctive cries of the street peddlers in the capital, varying in tone and timbre, are taken up by popular songsters who adapt these melodies to their own entertaining lyrics. This practice has become very popular today.

Gao Cheng (Song Dynasty) :
The Origins of Things

Street cries in the capital city are often imitated in every street and home. These adaptations are, in effect, songs combining the vendors' melodious chants with dubbed-in lyrics.

Wu Zimu (Song Dynasty):
Records of a Pipe Dream

九十九　賣冰 [1]

　　土人置窖冰，街坊擔賣，謂之涼冰。或雜以楊梅、桃子、花紅 [2] 之屬，俗呼冰楊梅、冰桃子。鮮魚市以之護魚，謂之冰鮮。

清　顧祿《清嘉錄》

【語譯】

　　本地人設置了儲冰窰，挑着擔子沿街叫賣，稱為涼冰。有的冰中還夾雜着楊梅、桃子、花紅等[水果]，俗稱冰楊梅、冰桃子。賣新鮮魚的市場上用冰來維持魚的 [新鮮]，這稱作冰鮮。

【註釋】

1. 賣冰：舊時南北兩地都市常見的商業景象。清代北京的賣冰人，手中持兩隻重疊着的小銅碟，碰擊發出"磕磕"的聲音，招呼別人來買。為防止冰融化，冰上常有棉絮遮蓋着。
2. 花紅：一種形似蘋果，但只有梅子般大小的水果。

258

99   Selling Ice[1]

Local people construct ice-cellars and sell ice carried on bamboo poles along the street. This sort of ice is called "cool ice". In this ice they sometimes put red bayberries, peaches or small apples. These confections are called, "iced bayberries", "iced peaches", etc. Ice is used to keep fish fresh in the market and this is called "ice-fresh".

Gu Lu (Qing Dynasty) :
Worthy Records of the Qing Dynasty

Notes:

1. Selling ice: a trade which existed in ancient times in both the northern and southern parts of China. In the Qing Dynasty ice vendors in Beijing clashed together two copper dishes in their hands to make a sound to attract buyers. To prevent the ice from melting, they covered it with layers of insulating cotton.

一百　接財神¹

　　五日為路頭神²誕辰，金鑼爆竹，牲醴畢陳，以爭先為利市，必早起迎之，謂之接路頭。案：《無錫縣志》："五路神姓何名五路，元末禦倭寇死，因祀之。"今俗所祀財神曰五路，似與此五路無涉。

　　　　　　　　　　　　清　顧祿《清嘉錄》

【語譯】

　　[夏曆正月]初五是財神的生日，[人們]敲鑼打鼓放爆竹，祭祀用的牲畜、甜酒等物陳設齊備。[民間]認為搶先[祭祀]是吉利的，故必定一早起牀迎接他，這稱為接財神。按：《無錫縣志》說："五路神姓何名五路，元代末年時因抵抗日本強盜而犧牲，所以[人們]祭祀他。"當今世俗所祭祀的財神也稱五路，似與這五路無關。

【註釋】

1. 接財神：每年夏曆正月初五，江南地區商店的店堂裏舉行接財神的儀式。據說因此可保證這年中生意興隆，財源茂盛。這是商家一年中重大的事件，此習俗流傳至今。
2. 路頭神：即財神，亦稱五路神。

100 Receiving the God of Wealth[1]

The fifth day of the first lunar month is the birth of the God of Wealth. People beat cymbals and gongs, light firecrackers, arrange sacrifices and offer sweet wine. Thinking priority beneficial and auspicious, they attempt to be first to hold this ceremony. People rise early to be the first to receive the god. According to <u>County Annals of Wuxi</u>, "Surnamed 'He' and named 'Wulu', the Wulu God died in a fight against Japanese bandits. People offer sacrifices to him." The God of Wealth whom people offer sacrifice to is also called Wulu, but it seems to have nothing to do with the Wulu God.

Gulu (Qing Dynasty) :
<u>Worthy Records of the Qing Dynasty</u>

Notes:

1. Receiving the God of Wealth: On January 5th of the lunar year, shops in the areas south of Yangtze River hold special receptions for the God of Wealth because people believe by doing so they can be assured of good business and plentiful profits in the following year. This occasion is an important yearly event and the custom is still practised today.

中國古代風俗一百則 = 100 ancient Chinese
customs / 厲振儀編著；姚紅英譯. -- 臺灣
初版. -- 臺北市：臺灣商務, 1997 [民86]
　　面 ；　公分. --（一百叢書：22）
　ISBN 957-05-1370-5（平裝）

1. 風俗習慣 - 中國

538.82　　　　　　　　　　　　85014352

一百叢書 ㉒

中國古代風俗一百則
100. ANCIENT CHINESS CUSTOMS

定價新臺幣 300 元

編 著 者　厲　振　儀
英 譯 者　姚　　紅
　責任編輯　金　　堅

出 版 者
印 刷 所　臺灣商務印書館股份有限公司
　　　　　臺北市 10036 重慶南路 1 段 37 號
　　　　　電話：(02)23116118．23115638
　　　　　傳眞：(02)23710274．23701091
　　　　　讀者服務專線：080056196
　　　　　E-mail:cptw@ms12.hinet.net
　　　　　郵政劃撥：0000165 — 1 號
　　　　　出版事業
　　　　　登 記 證：局版北市業字第 993 號

‧ 1996 年 9 月香港初版
‧ 1997 年 3 月臺灣初版第一次印刷
‧ 2000 年 7 月臺灣初版第二次印刷
本書經商務印書館（香港）有限公司授權出版

ISBN　957-05-1370-5（平裝）　　　　b 56427110